I read your book, ALL ABOUT GOALS AND HOW TO ACHIEVE THEM, with enthusiasm. It is a great book—logical, sensible, practical and very interesting. I marked passage after passage and hope you won't mind if I quote you quite a lot.

—Dr. Norman Vincent Peale

ALL ABOUT GOALS

AND HOW TO ACHIEVE THEM

JACK ENSIGN ADDINGTON

DeVorss & Company
P.O. Box 550
Marina del Rey, California 90294

Library of Congress Catalog Number: 77-080016

ISBN: O-87516-237-1

First Printing 1977 - 10,000
Second Printing 1978 - 20,000
Third Printing 1981 - 20,000
Fourth Printing 1984 - 10,000
Fifth Printing 1986 - 10,000
Sixth Printing 1989 - 5,000

Printed in the United States of America

To my wife, Cornelia, whose ideas and persistence have made this book possible.

Books by Jack Ensign Addington

YOUR NEEDS MET
I AM THE WAY
THE PERFECT POWER WITHIN YOU
THE JOY OF MEDITATION
ALL ABOUT PROSPERITY AND HOW YOU CAN
  PROSPER
DRAWING THE LARGER CIRCLE
THE WONDER-WORKING POWER OF GOD

With Cornelia Addington

YOUR NEEDS MET
I AM THE WAY
THE PERFECT POWER WITHIN YOU
THE JOY OF MEDITATION
ALL ABOUT PROSPERITY AND HOW YOU CAN
  PROSPER
DRAWING THE LARGER CIRCLE

Books may be ordered from Abundant Living Foundation, Box 100, San Diego, CA 92138. Current price list available upon request.
Distributed to the book trade by DeVorss & Company, Box 550, Marina del Rey, CA 90294.

Inspirational

We grow to the stature of our goals. Without a goal to keep us trying, our souls atrophy like unused muscles.

Frank Laubach

Many men and women fail in life, not for lack of ability, or brains, or even courage, but simply because they have never organized their energies around a central goal.

Elmer Wheeler

CONTENTS

There Is a System That Really Works
We Had Touched on a Law of Mind
An Overview of Goal Achievement
You Can't Travel in Two Directions at Once
Ten Goals at Once? Yes!
Goals Should Be Thought of as Already Accomplished
Don't Lift the Lid and Let the Steam Escape
Value of Writing Down Goals
Are Material Desires Wrong?
Claim Your Goal
Achievers Are Goal-Setters
Set New Goals Each Year
The Art of Goal-Setting Can Change Your Life

Goal-Achievement on the Larger Scale
Proof That the System Works
Don't Accept Defeat Under Any Circumstances
Goals Program of Tremendous Help
Finds All Phases of Life Changing for the Better
Her Goals Were Realized in Perfect Ways for Her
The Unseen Factory of Life
Some Goals Achieved Quickly, Others Take Longer
See the Finished Product and It Will Come From
    Somewhere

Jack La Lanne's Unusual Goal
Author Too Young to Quit Writing at 87
The Incredible Career of Grandma Moses
Some Goals Sound Crazy to Others—So What!
Only Your Own Mental Barriers Stand in the Way

A Summary

INTRODUCTION

This book could be the most important book you will ever read. <u>Why</u>? Because life is a series of goals and there are various techniques for setting and achieving goals. There are natural laws that need to be known and applied if we would consistently realize our goals.

Every person is a goal-setter whether or not he realizes it. Most of us are working in the dark. We wonder why some goals are achieved and others not. This book will help you set goals intelligently and wisely — goals that are legitimate, realistic and attainable. The achieving of these goals can be immensely rewarding to you. I hope so

Some goals are major objectives. Some are minor objectives. All are important in making up the pattern of our lives. Some goals are day-to-day goals. Some are hour-to-hour goals. Each one is a <u>step in the journey through life.</u> Although goal-setting is as natural as breathing, few people know how to achieve their goals. Many people, unwittingly, set negative goals and then wonder why their lives are filled with negative experiences. Therefore, it becomes very important to learn the pitfalls of goal-setting. The person who misses the

13

mark each time he sets a goal is either setting goals that are out of tune with his life, or he has the wrong *attitude* about his goals.

This is a very simple book. It goes right to the point: *how to set goals and how to achieve them.* Setting and achieving goals are the most important activities in anyone's life. One who does not understand successful goal-achievement becomes disappointed and frustrated. The successful goal-achiever finds health, wealth and happiness.

Setting and achieving goals becomes an art and a science when one realizes that goal-achievement is governed by definite mental laws and not by luck or chance. Everyone should know these laws and how they work. Everyone should know the penalties of misusing the laws, as well as the successes that come with applying them wisely and properly. *good adj.*

This book is designed to present various techniques that have proved effective in using the laws of mind for goal-achievement. The pitfalls have been pointed out with examples and instructions as to how to avoid them.

Some people achieve their goals in spite of tremendous handicaps. There is a woman in Jacksonville, Florida, who, without hands or feet, has achieved great success in painting greeting cards, holding the brush in her teeth. She had a goal and believed in it. A long-distance runner, afflicted with polio in childhood so that he could hardly walk, took up running to get strength in his legs

attitude is everything

very important

Mind over matter

nice ring to it

and became a champion. He had a goal and believed in it. Demosthenes, the stammerer of antiquity, wanted to become an orator and practiced with pebbles in his mouth. Was it luck that he did become one of the great orators of all time? History has numerous stories of great philanthropists born in the slums and raised in poverty, who acquired great wealth and wound up giving away millions of dollars. A man who had no formal education and lacked an environment for learning, became so well educated that at the age of 35 he became chancellor of a great university. Why did these people succeed in the face of such tremendous odds while others who seemed to be favored with every advantage missed the mark completely?

The late Maxwell Maltz, a prominent New York plastic surgeon, and author of PSYCHOCYBERNETICS, found that when a person had plastic surgery, improving his image, he tended to change his personality to fit the new face. Does this not cause you to wonder why that person did not change his personality even before the surgery? I assure you, there is a reason. It can work both ways.

A prominent medical doctor, specializing in cancer cure, teaches his patients to mentally see the cancerous area completely healed. He has them imagine new cells replacing the old cancerous cells. He has them quietly meditating on this healed area each day and works with them on

The mind can heal

success

mind over matter

overcoming the mental and emotional feelings that contributed to the illness. They build new attitudes that cause healing. Is this not a form of goal-setting? It works.

A salesman returned to his office day after day without making a single sale. He found it difficult to understand how his colleagues could bring in five to ten orders a day. It didn't seem fair. And then, he learned the secret: a positive technique for goal-setting and goal-achievement. Now he leads in sales week after week.

I could go on and on telling you of instances of people who have changed their lives dramatically when they learned how to set goals for themselves and believe in those goals. Why is it that some people are able to do this and others not? Do the goal-achievers know something that the others don't know? Why do some arrive at the top and others never get off first base? Well, that's what this book is all about. It will show you how anyone can dramatically change his life through an understanding of goal-achieving.

The techniques in this book are not just for salesmen. They can improve the business of living for anyone. We are all setting goals continually. We might as well start achieving them! Nothing can keep us from it once we understand how to set realistic and legitimate goals and use the power of the mind to achieve them.

Jack Ensign Addington

Chapter I

GOAL-ACHIEVING SEEMS LIKE
MAGIC, BUT IT ISN'T

There is an old saying, *Man seeks to satisfy his desires with the least amount of effort.* There are those who claim this to be a law of life and that this law accounts for man's inventive drives, his continual urge toward short cuts in every phase of life, as well as the childish desire to have his every wish come true. Who didn't at some stage in life desire an Aladdin's lamp to rub to have one's every wish immediately appear before his eyes.

It is apparently man's nature to be looking for what would seem like magic in achieving the little things and the big things of life. Even life itself seems to be magical. We all realize that there are natural laws with which we must work in agreement to bring about the magical results. The achieving of goals appears to be the result of just such a magical process, but we know that behind it all is something at work which we can utilize for our advantage, gain and pleasure. How do we do this? We are about to find out.

There Is a System That Really Works

Years ago, when I was the minister of a large city church, my wife and I struggled with a problem that seemed absolutely insurmountable. At that time the congregation was growing very fast. We needed at least 20 ushers for our Sunday service and we had only one man who seemed to want the job. He was probably the last person we would have chosen to usher. He was a back-slapper who greeted each person in a loud voice, and who insisted on wearing his hat while he ushered. He seemed to have a great number of friends in our congregation, so we were reluctant to do anything that would offend him. He had taken over the job when we started the church and he continually informed us that no one else wanted to usher. He was such a tyrant that he scared everyone, even us. Worse than that, he appeared to be freezing everyone else out. It may sound unimportant to you today, but, at that time, it seemed to us like an impossible situation. We prayed over it. We stewed over it. We came to feel completely stymied.

In desperation, we decided to try something. We wrote a letter to the universal mind power. We wrote out our needs and desires regarding the perfect staff of ushers: a corps of 20 ushers who would meet before the church service and meditate together, a closely knit group that would be a real strength in the church. Call it what you will, it was a goal. After we had written out this goal in detail, we gave thanks as if it were already accomplished, folded the letter and put it in a leather jewel box. Connie and I promised each other that we would think of this need as already met and stop worrying about it.

Some months later we had occasion to look in the leather box and there was our letter to universal mind power. We opened it and read it aloud. And, what do you know! It had happened. We now had over 20 men who were not only doing a beautiful job of ushering each Sunday morning but were the nucleus of a men's club which had become a real strength in the church. The back slapper had become offended by what someone had said to him, so he started going elsewhere.

We Had Touched On a Law of Mind

The words, *conceive, believe, receive* are inscribed on the gold medallion worn by many students of Abundant Living, and are the abbreviation of a very important law. We call it the law of goal-achievement. For, it is a law of mind that *that which you can conceive of, believe in, and confidently expect for yourself, must necessarily become your experience.*[1] You see, when we had been able to release our need and stop thinking about it as something we lacked, it all happened so easily that we had even forgotten we ever had

[1]Jack Addington, *PSYCHOGENESIS, Everything Begins in Mind,* (New York: Dodd Mead & Co., 1971).

such a problem. Once we had entrusted our goal to the universal mind power, we had a new attitude, and according to the creative process working through all of life, our goal was met.

From then on, we wrote out our goals and put them in the brown leather jewel box. Every Thanksgiving we made a little ceremony of opening the box and reading our goals. It was really exciting. Without exception, they had been achieved! There was something about putting our desires down on paper that helped us release them. When we put them in the box, *believing that they were going to be accomplished,* they were realized in our experience. The dates now go back 20 years. Many who read this book will recognize our goals, having seen them come into being. Each one of our books, now into many printings, was once a goal in the jewel box. Every time we read the old goals again we are amazed how accurately they have been filled. There is really nothing superstitious about this. It works according to a law: *that which you can conceive of, believe in, and confidently expect for yourself, must necessarily become your experience.*

An Overview of Goal-Achievement

The following observations, questions, and answers serve as an overview of goal-setting and goal-achievement. The reader will observe that he can begin right now to succeed in goal-achievement, for the laws that apply are totally concrete.

You Can't Travel in Two Directions at Once

Singleness of purpose is necessary to activate the law. You cannot hedge your bets. You see, most of us straddle the fence, keeping one foot on each side. We want to believe that we will receive our heart's desire, but we can't quite believe that we will. We hedge our goal by thinking, "If I don't get it, I can always make some other arrangement." As a matter of self-protection, so we won't be too disappointed, we plan a compromise, which is really another goal. We wind up looking in two directions at once. Have you ever tried going in two directions at once? It isn't easy! There is a Bible quotation that says it all:

> *But let him ask in faith, nothing wavering. For he that wavereth is like a wave of the sea driven with the wind and tossed. For let not that man think that he shall receive anything of the Lord. A double minded man is unstable in all his ways.* (Ja. 1:6-8)

faith not wavering

The shortest distance between two points is still a straight line. Avoid unnecessary detours in your thinking. My good friend, the late Dr. Frederick Bailes, called it "straight-line thinking." We should, therefore, give single-minded attention to that which we really want to achieve. The simple law of cause and effect assures us: *"That to which we give our attention is going to become our experience."* Are we thinking of ourselves as weak and sickly—or strong and healthy? Are we thinking of ourselves as unfortunate, unlucky, subject to failure? It is up to us to set the kind of a goal in mind we really want to experience and then keep the eye on the goal.

According to Webster, a goal is *the end which a person intends to reach or attain.* Call them goals, or objectives, it makes no difference. The important thing is to mentally keep moving toward the target.

Ten Goals at Once? Yes!

Does one scatter his fire by having ten goals at once? No. Emile Zola had three goals: to plant a tree; to have a child; to write a book. He accomplished all three and many more. There was no conflict in these goals. The thing we have to watch out for is having goals that are in conflict with each other. Example: One cannot be married and single at the same time, although some today are making a stab at it. There are those who claim that they want to be healthy, while, secretly, entertaining a goal of remaining ill to gain attention.

Goals Should Be Thought of as Already Accomplished

Does that mean that we are never to think about them? No, you can think about them if you think of them as already accomplished. When you think of your goal as already accomplished, release it to the creative process of the mind. Don't "worry" your goals. Never, never allow yourself to feel anxious about them. This will impede your progress. It is important to trust the universal mind power to draw to your goal all that is needed to bring it into manifestation.

I'll have to work on that.

Don't Lift the Lid and Let the Steam Escape

Should we not discuss our goals with others? Maybe

It is well to keep your personal goals a secret between you and the universal mind. There is power in your belief and enthusiasm for your goal. Others may not share your enthusiasm. If you discuss your goals with others, they may try to talk you out of them and cause you to have doubts. Goal sharing partnerships and couples working toward a common goal are exceptions. The point is, don't lift the lid and let the steam escape!

Value of Writing Down Goals

Do you have to write your goals down on a sheet of paper and put them in a box?

No, but it surely helps. It finalizes the desire. It makes you feel a sense of release. You are doing something about it and now you can release it. Once you have found how well the system works, a new confidence is established.

A system is what I need. An organized way to accomplish my goals.

Are Material Desires Wrong?

Is it wrong to have desires for material things?

It has been said: *thoughts are things.* Material things are the outer evidence of a change in consciousness. As long as you do not try to achieve your goals at the expense of another, as long as your desires hurt no one else, I believe that there is nothing wrong with desiring things.

Claim Your Goal

What do you mean when you say to "claim your goal"?

There is no virtue in being timid where life is concerned. Life will work with you according to your demands upon it. To claim is to seek to obtain by virtue of authority or right. If your goal is legitimate and realistic, then you should claim it in Mind as if it were an accomplished fact. You either claim your goal or you disclaim it. There is no in-between. If you claim it, you accept it and possess it in Mind. If you disclaim it, you renounce or repudiate your right to the goal. Life will take you at your own evaluation.

Achievers Are Goal-Setters

What about people who seem to achieve whatever they set out to accomplish and yet are not conscious of having goals?

When we set out to accomplish something we *are* setting a goal. The desire to accomplish sets a goal in Mind. When the objective is achieved it proves that goal-setting works. There are those who are such orderly thinkers that they have no need to write things down in order to clarify their thoughts.

Set New Goals Each Year

Why is it a good idea to set new goals at the beginning of a new year? answer?

When one sets new goals at the beginning of a year, he then can check to see how many goals were attained in the year past. cool

He can look at the goals that were not achieved and ask himself a few questions about them. analyze

Were they goals he really wanted to attain? Did he doubt? Was there a false motive? Were the goals realistic? There are many reasons why goals are not achieved and they are important to understand if one would be a goal-achiever. Keeping a list will give one a check chart and help one evaluate his thinking. step #7.

The Art of Goal-Setting Can Change Your Life

Can one really change his life by understanding and applying the techniques of goal-achievement?

I don't know!

Yes. Once a person knows how to select his goals wisely and understands what takes place in mind in bringing about the achieving of his goals, then his whole life can take an about-face. He can become constructive and affirmative in his thinking and in his approach to making his goals. To be able to set goals and focus the attention necessary to bring about their fulfillment is a great achievement, and one that will bring much happiness with a sense of dominion and inner power that brings a person a deep satisfaction. In short, the understanding of making goals can bring health, wealth and happiness into the life of any person who is willing to do something about it.

Sounds like this is going to work.

Chapter II

A FAR-REACHING EXPERIMENT
IN GOAL-ACHIEVING

Several years ago I said to my wife, "If only people could find how easy it is to achieve goals the way we do! Too bad everyone doesn't know our secret!"

Her reply was, "Why don't we tell them our secret?" The more I thought about it, the more I realized she was right.

Christmas 1974 seemed a good time to share this idea with my readers and radio listeners. What better Christmas gift could I send them — one that could be used from then on in answer to any need that might arise — the gift of a lifetime, really.

We had found that when we wrote out our goals and put them in the brown leather jewel box, *believing that we would receive them*, they were, without exception, made manifest in our experience. If it worked so well for us, this system of goal-achievement, why wouldn't it be a boon to everyone? There was nothing superstitious about

27

it, it was simply a matter of placing an order with Life and releasing it to the Law of Life. It was plain that our little brown jewel box, already over-flowing with our family goals, could never be stretched to accommodate thousands of goal sheets. So we found at a toy store a large "treasure chest" to be the goal box for our larger family.

Goal-Achievement on the Larger Scale

You've heard it said, *the proof of the pudding is in the eating,* and this experiment turned out to be a good example. We sent out 12,000 goal sheets to be filled out and mailed back to us. We promised to return them the following Thanksgiving so that the goal-achievers could see with their own eyes how it works. The idea caught on. Several thousand goal sheets were returned. As we placed them in the "treasure chest" we released them to the universal mind power. We did not read the goals because we consider a person's goals a very private matter. "Remember," we wrote back, "once you have written out your goals and sent them in to us you are not to worry about them any more. They are to be completely released by you. If you are tempted to think about your goals, think of them as already accomplished in mind. Don't limit your goals. Your goals can be for health, happiness, prosperity, harmony in the home, wisdom, guidance, or *anything.* Nothing is too good for you."

Power lies in the mind

Proof That the System Works

Long before Thanksgiving we began to receive reports that the goals had already been achieved. Many released their goals so completely that they forgot what they had asked for! Therefore, when we returned the sheets at Thanksgiving, and what a job it was, we received hundreds of letters from those who had not realized until then that their goals had indeed come true in surprising ways.

Don't Accept Defeat Under
Any Circumstances Always be successful

How I wish I could give you all the reports that came to us. What interesting stories they would make! For instance, a couple in San Jose, California, writes:

> We are so excited! Many of the goals we sent you last November are now coming true. We asked in those goals for a good business site for the manufacturing of adobes and also for the purpose of raising animals. We asked for a house with four bedrooms and a greenhouse. Well, we have found just that. We found a 65-acre farm in the hills of San Juan. It has a well with enough water for everything we want to do. We also found a four-bedroom house in the town of San Juan with a greenhouse in the big spacious backyard we so wanted for our kids.

Goals Program of Tremendous Help

Here's a letter from Texas:

> *I'm sorry I haven't written you to tell you that every need I had in 1974 has been met. The Goals Program has been such a tremendous help in my life.*

Finds All Phases of Life Changing for Better

I like what this person says:

> *All phases of my life are changing for the better. Some areas show an amazing improvement—just amazing!*
>
> *In the harmony with others department, things got horribly worse for a while, and I had to go all-out to become more harmonious. It works, of course, when we work at it. And I had to work at it in order to stay in my beloved art class. My progress in art has taken off like a rocket. I see, as do others, the vast improvement in my paintings. Two different people have asked to buy from me. Today a man is buying two! My goals met!*

[handwritten in margin: A goal can be for anything: art, life, job, relationship]

Her Goals Were Realized in Perfect Ways for Her

A woman from Berkeley, California writes:

So many good things have happened! I have been promoted and given two raises on my job. The work is great! I'm surprised by reports that most people don't enjoy their work. Fortunately most people in my office are happy. Perhaps that is why the surroundings are pleasant despite government-office-type decor.

And then she adds: *"I'm growing upward and outward. Many thanks."*

The Unseen Factory of Life

Here's a woman who has her own goals box to help her release her goals into Life:

I fixed up my own goals box and have been putting my goals in it. I started it last month, and some have already been met. Now my husband is using it, too.

I once heard a sermon entitled "Heaven—Unseen Factory of Life." I keep the goals box in our bedroom, and every time I think of the goals I've put in there, or every time my eyes fall on the box, I think to myself, well, those goals are all being filled in the perfect way at the "Factory"!

Some Goals Achieved Quickly, Others Take Longer

Some goals seem to be quickly reached, while

others take longer to take form, as this woman in Oregon has discovered:

> *I sent in four goals when you requested we make known our sincere desires, and that at the end of the year you would mail them back to us so that we could see how they had all come true. Well, two of my four goals are already fulfilled.*

See the Finished Product and It Will Come From Somewhere

Even the children discovered the principle behind goal-achievement. A grandmother in Lakewood, Colorado writes:

> *This was a beautiful summer. My grandchildren met once a week and listened to the cassettes on THE PERFECT POWER WITHIN YOU,[1] then had a short discussion about it. One little fellow, 11 years, has such faith, he is a pleasure.*
>
> *We were all delighted when his greatest wish came true on his birthday. He plays the guitar, but wanted a complete drum set. With things as they were financially, no one could see two or three hundred dollars for*

[1]Jack and Cornelia Addington, *THE PERFECT POWER WITHIN YOU*, (Marina del Rey, CA.: DeVorss & Co., 1974).

The Future is in the child

one, but that didn't bother Jess. He kept saying, "See the finished product and it will come from somewhere." Well, the week before his birthday, his daddy, who has a small band, mentioned this to some of the gang. An old friend who used to be a drummer but had to give it up because of health, sold his complete professional drum set for $100.00. Jess' dream came true.

Like Holding Up a Cup to Be Filled

There's a lesson for all of us here. Sometimes even before the physical evidence, we know that our goals are on the way:

So many things have happened I could not possibly relate them all to you. I used to have periodic depressions that have virtually vanished. Oh, I have those "arid periods" now and then, when inspiration and enthusiasm are not forthcoming. During those times I remember my favorite line, "Desire in the heart is God tapping at the door of consciousness with His infinite supply." If the desire is there, then it is certainly possible to achieve it. And those arid periods last only hours, at the very most. I found that depression was merely faith in the wrong direction —inability to reach a goal.

The Heaven Factory of life

I KNOW my goals are already accomplished and physical manifestation isn't far away. How true it is—we have only ourselves to change.

Daily I ask for guidance. It is, truly, like holding up a cup to be filled. Amazing how much guidance—how many new ideas come —when you ask for them.

It wasn't long before we had another letter from this young lady:

Have been meaning to write, but have been caught up in the recent changes in my life. First of all, I now have the ideal job I've been seeking for several years. It fits exactly the specifications in my list of goals.

Editing (which I have long desired).

Close to home (10 minutes, as opposed to years of hour-each-way commuting).

Flexible hours (for the time being, I have elected to work only 20 hours a week).

Salary (this is the clincher—I'm now making the same amount for 20 hours' work as I previously did for 40).

Opportunity (I'm learning new things every day!).

This schedule has allowed me to spend more time with my family, which was also a goal.

This all seems truly a miracle. Truly, everything does come in its proper season if we "keep the faith."

GOD

Dreams Come True in Wonderful Ways

We are truly happy to be a part of this goal-fulfillment story:

> My heart's desire and last year's goals became a reality. I was married March 21st to a wonderful man.
>
> Sometimes when our prayer works the way we ask and it is so much more, we are utterly flabbergasted. At least I was. I had asked, "We shall know each other when we meet." We met at a Senior Citizen's dance, February 14th, and he looked at me across the hall and told his housekeeper whom he had taken to the dance, "I'm going to marry her." A week later he proposed and we were married on the 21st of March. Everything is beautiful. He is 73 and I am 60—very young, both of us.

good for them

their life begins

Romance, Business Success, a New Home—All Goals Achieved

Romance, business success, a new home? It doesn't matter. If you can sincerely believe in your goal and confidently expect it to materialize, it will, as the following letters prove.

A woman from Bellingham, Washington writes:

> I'm happily living in a condominium located on a half-acre of park-like grounds, after the sale of my seven-room home which

Great, but tell me how to do it

had been my home for the past 15 years. The sale of the home, the disposition of excess furniture, appliances and "things" were made in perfect order. Perfecting the change was my goal for this year and it came about sooner than I expected.

Here's a letter from a goal-achiever in Chicago:

I am most happy to report that I am now working full-time. After my letter to you, I was contacted by a friend who was instrumental in helping me secure fulltime work. I am working at a job that I truly love. This position is better than anything I had imaged. I am so thankful that I can hardly contain myself. Everything about my goal—location, atmosphere, pay, bonus, and work are ideal for me.

Here's a goal-achiever who sets mind stretchers and expects the best:

It really appears that this GOAL SETTING HAS GREAT POWER. Remember, in 1974 I set a goal to get a new home that I liked. I GOT IT.

In 1975 I set two goals: (1) To have an income of $2,000 a month or more, and (2) To get a fine husband for my daughter, Melody, who is beautiful and 25.

WELL, MIRACLE! MIRACLE! MIRACLE! BOTH GOALS HAVE BECOME A

Miracle?
or the system

REALITY. Melody is now engaged to a millionaire in his mid-30's, a six-foot tall, handsome man, who made $1,500,000 in one year, is a Mormon Priest, a scratch golfer, and a wonderful sweet man. My daughter and he are deeply in love. The wedding is set for April 2, 1977, probably at my home in my garden. *A lot of money then*

I have made over $25,000 this year—over $2,000 a month. Of course, this is not $2,000 a month from investments that pay without work, but it is good. Next year looks much better.

Finally, this letter from Chicago:

I was delighted to receive my goal sheet back from you, and to report that seven out of 12 goals have been realized. The other five I neglected to truly work at. The really important ones, though, are among the "Mission Accomplished" ones.

1976 has truly been an eventful year, one this family will long remember. In addition to the family's surgeries and marriage and job accomplishments, I have become knowledgeable in an area of my work in which I was previously somewhat uncertain; a friend did get the promotion he felt was rightfully his; in a settlement concerning the accident my daughter had in Mexico, she was awarded an amount greater than any expectations and without a court case; and my younger daughter received an engagement ring for Christmas which brought her much happiness.

I approach the new year in an attitude of gratitude.

I find it hard to know where to stop. Each letter is a glimpse into someone's life, a life that has been enriched through this goal-setting plan. I've come to see that the letter I mailed to my readers and radio listeners, Christmas 1974, was the best Christmas gift I could have given. What's more, it started a precedent. Now we have a Goals Program every year and, as each one's confidence grows, the stories get better and better as more and more goals are realized.

[handwritten in left margin: Why money first? 3]

[handwritten note: So far I have only heard success stories. Tell me how to do it. I am very happy for these people, but I need to know how to achieve my goals.]

Chapter III

THE FACTORY OF YOUR MIND

It has been said that the two greatest discoveries made by man were the discovery of fire and the discovery of the wheel. It is true that these two discoveries opened the way for the emergence of civilized man.

The greatest discovery of recent history has been the science of mind and how to use it. It is only in the last century that we have begun to define the specialized uses of both the conscious and subconscious mind. These are not two separate minds, but the activities of universal mind individualized in each one of us.

It Works for Us Even as We Sleep

It is astonishing, almost unbelievable, how the subconscious mind works for us. A family story illustrates my point. We are living in a *do-it-yourself* era. If you want a thing done, unless the job is worth a great deal of money, no one is interested. It is up to you to find a way to do it.

39 money, money, money

The story happened this way. First, we put in air-conditioning. Since we live in an upstairs condominium, the unit had to go on the roof right above the front door. It looked unsightly. There must be some way to hide it, we reasoned. This was a challenge for my wife who was formerly an interior decorator. She thought about it for several days and came up with a sketch of a wooden screen to put in front of the unit. She thought we could just buy a few feet of fencing and have it installed. It wasn't that simple. We called in a contractor who sharpened his pencil and gave us an estimate. Before he got through adding up materials, labor, paint, insurance, etc., it was like putting in the air-conditioning all over again— $259.00 for just four feet of fence. By then, we had thought it through so many times we felt as if we had already done the job.

"Why not?" We'd do it ourselves. It would be easy.

So we bought $26.00 worth of materials and congratulated ourselves on our ingenuity—that is, until we thought about it further. I woke up one night with the awful thought: "How am I ever going to get those six foot long 4x4's up the ladder, onto the roof?" I had thought of tieing a rope around them and dragging them up, but there was no way to hold those heavy posts in place. (My wife had already informed me that she would not be of much help to me on the roof. She would not

Never is (handwritten marginalia)

be going up on the roof at all.) I, therefore, woke her with this problem.

"That's one for the subconscious mind," she countered happily and went back to sleep. Sure enough, at 6:00 o'clock the next morning she came up with the answer. "It came to me as I woke up!" she cried triumphantly. "I saw in my mind's eye a whole table of pulleys, pulleys of every size and color. All we need is that long rope that we got to give the dog obedience lessons, and one of those pulleys I saw on that table, and we're in! You can do it! I can hold the rope from down on the porch!"

This had to have come from the universal subconscious mind for my wife had never been aware of pulleys. It really was amazing and, of course, it was the perfect answer. We bought a pulley for $1.89 and I easily pulled the post up onto the roof and into place while she held the rope from below. Now we have a most attractive screen in front of our air-conditioning unit, and great satisfaction in having "done it" ourselves. *appreciate it more*

We have used this principle, asking the subconscious mind to work for us while we sleep, over and over again to find the right house for us, the right automobile, right answers to many problems. It works every time. Try it yourself. Every need we have in life is an opportunity to set a goal and let the subconscious mind achieve it for us, through us. *So we are working hard, but not working at all!*

Subconcious Mind Power

Setting a goal creates a mold into which the energy of life flows. We live in a vast sea of mind, a plastic substance, out of which all creation is made. Sir Arthur Eddington called it *mind stuff.* This fluidic substance is as ready and willing to flow into our mental molds as the sea is ready to flow in and fill every little depression on the shore. When we make small goals we provide a small mold to be filled. Our great goals provide great molds which are just as eagerly filled by *mind stuff.* . . .

Let Us See How the Mind Works

Each one of us, at his point of awareness, individualizes and uses the one mind. We are not separate from it. The one mind which we all use has been likened to a vast underground spring which wells up to the surface wherever there is an opening. As we think, we use the one mind at our own point of expression.

The brain is the instrument of mind. Of itself, it does not think. Just as your television set does not originate its programs, mind thinks through the brain which acts as a receiving set.

The conscious and subconscious functions of mind have been compared by psychologists to an iceberg. A vast portion of the iceberg is hidden under the water. Only one-ninth appears above the surface. That part which is visible compares to the conscious mind, that little portion of which we are aware. But the great activity is hidden beneath the surface. It is sometimes called the unconscious mind. how much does it do?

The conscious mind directs, chooses, analyzes, envisions, imagines and reasons both inductively and deductively. The subconscious mind is *subject* to the conscious mind. It can reason only deductively, taking the premises given it by the conscious mind. It makes no difference what kind of premises they are. The subconscious mind can be compared to a factory. The factory does not question whether or not it receives good designs from the design department, but goes to work on the design it has been given. In the same way, your subconscious mind does not concern itself over the kind of goals you give it. It goes to work on the negative as well as the affirmative goals, carrying out your orders with precision. well oiled-machine

Because you are a part of the universal mind, at your point of use you have the resources of the Infinite at your disposal. No one said it better than Ralph Waldo Emerson in his essay on history:

> *There is one mind common to all individual men. Every man* is an inlet to the same and to all of the same. He that is once admitted to the right of reason is made a freeman of the whole estate. What Plato has thought, he may think; what a saint has felt,*

**man here refers to generic man which includes woman.*

Miss Resnik

(margin annotations: "Just does it", "a lot of comparision")

he may feel; what at any time has befallen
any man, he can understand. Who hath ac-
cess to this universal mind is a party to all
that is or can be done.

Each one of us approaches the universal mind
at his own point of consciousness. Each one is an
inlet to all of it. Only man (woman) is able to
direct the activity of the subconscious mind know-
ingly and with the realization of what he is doing.
No other part of life has this ability. Only man is
aware that as he thinks a thought consciously and
lets it rest in his subconscious mind, this thought
will emerge in manifestation as the outer expression of that thought. This is the creative process —
from the invisible world of mind *into* the visible
outer expression. The law of life draws everything
together to perfect your dream. I do not know how
the subconscious mind does this. I only know it
happens. It is part of the mystery of creation.

Sometimes the Subconscious Mind
Needs to Be Convinced
That We Mean Business

If the order you give your subconscious mind is
a right-about-face from your previous direction, it
may take repetition to convince your subconscious
mind that you really mean the order you are now
giving it. An example of this came across my desk
recently.

(handwritten margin note: reverse Phycology)

One of my radio listeners heard me talk about how to stop smoking. She sent for my article, YES, YOU CAN STOP SMOKING, offered over the broadcast. In it, I suggested that it is imperative to use affirmative orders, not negative orders, in giving direction to the subconscious mind. This she did. Every time she lit a cigarette she told herself, "I am free from the smoking habit." She laughed to herself as over and over she said the words, "I am free from the smoking habit!" And then, one day she picked up a cigarette, tapped it on her cigarette case, put it to her lips and lit it. And then, she put her lighted cigarette down on the ash tray. She *was* free. She never smoked again. The subconscious mind had followed the direction she had so faithfully given it and had brought about her freedom from an annoying habit.

Smoking and Goals

Suppose your goal is to stop smoking. How do you go about it? *(handwritten: Alot of people's goal)*

Here we come back to self-identification. What do you believe about yourself, think about yourself, identify with yourself? Is it being a smoker? Then, you literally say over and over to yourself, "I am a smoker." But if you would like to discontinue smoking, you have to give your subconscious mind a new and positive order. This order can be in the form of a change of self-identification.

(handwritten: Personal)

Think to yourself, "I am a non-smoker." Imagine yourself saying to your friends who offer you a cigarette, "No, thank you, I don't smoke."

It makes no difference whether you continue to smoke, but keep identifying yourself with the idea, "I am a non-smoker." At just the right time you will become that ideal image with which you have identified yourself. *You will be a non-smoker.*

Dr. S. I. Hayakawa, in an article entitled "How To Stop Smoking," told how he used this affirmative approach. For weeks he kept saying to himself, "I am a non-smoker." He said it took him six weeks to change his concept of himself from smoker to non-smoker. One day, six weeks after he had started, he suddenly realized that he had indeed changed his concept of himself, and that he now was a non-smoker. He never smoked after that.

This change of concept was the goal that Dr. Hayakawa had established in his consciousness.

The Where of It

Where are goals set and achieved?
In the mind of the person setting and achieving the goals. When you change your mind you change your experience. Habits are not something "out there" but "in here."

Choice and Goals

How does the conscious mind know what orders to give the subconscious mind?

The conscious mind has the power of choice. The conscious mind can use all of its powers of mental investigation, analysis, study and weighing of facts to determine the choice of the goal to be set. Once the choice is made, the subconscious mind will accept that choice as a direction. The potency that the subconscious mind will put into reproducing that choice will depend upon the intensity of the feeling, the intensity of the desire, the intensity of the acceptance, and the persistence and perseverance of the conscious mind. This does not mean that we have to mentally force something to happen. We are not talking about willpower. The right use of the will is to keep the attention on the objective.

Self-Direction and Goals

How is it that one can change his life by changing his thoughts?

By what is known as the law of self-direction. Each one has the power to direct his conscious mind in such a way that he gives orders to the subconscious mind. The subconscious mind knows only to take orders from the conscious mind and carry out these orders with precision and exactitude. Therefore, when you set a goal, you are setting the direction of your conscious mind, and this becomes an order to the subconscious mind. The direction that you give the conscious mind becomes the law of your life.

Hard Work and Goals

I received this question in a letter:

"I set goals and then work my head off, but I don't make them. Then some dude comes along who sets higher goals than I and doesn't work nearly as hard, and makes his goals easily. What's wrong with me?"

[handwritten margin note: we're common question]

[handwritten margin note: That's]

Working hard is relative. Some people work hard and misdirect their energies. Others channel their energies with more ease and better direction, accomplishing their goals easily. The golfer who hits a beautiful golf shot will knock the ball "a mile." It looks easy because his timing is perfect. Another person's timing will be off, making everything he does appear strenuous. Our first goal should be to work in an easy, well-directed, well-timed manner. This means to take all strenuous push, forced exertion and hurry out of the action. To be graceful means to flow with life, and our work should be graceful.

The key to exceptional production is the word *let*. Set your goal and then *let* the creativity, the energy and the intelligence of life flow through you to bring the goal into manifestation. This does not mean that you sit and do nothing, but it does mean that you move toward your goal in a relaxed, well-directed manner.

[handwritten note: Relax … have fun]

Goal-Setting and Achieving
More Than Mechanical

Is goal-achieving a strictly mechanical thing?
No, feeling plays a very important part in goal-achievement.

The following excerpt from FEELING IS THE SECRET by Neville illustrates the importance of feeling in goal-achievement:

The subconscious does not originate ideas but accepts as true those which the conscious mind feels to be true and in a way known only to itself objectifies the accepted ideas. Therefore, through his power to imagine and feel and his freedom to choose the idea he will entertain, man has control over creation. Control of the subconscious is accomplished through control of your ideas and feelings.

The mechanism of creation is hidden in the very depth of the subconscious, the female aspect or womb of creation. The subconscious transcends reason and is independent of induction. It contemplates a feeling as a fact existing within itself and on this assumption proceeds to give expression to it. The creative process begins with an idea and its cycle runs its course as a feeling and ends in a volition to act. forced?

Ideas are impressed on the subconscious through the medium of feeling. No idea can

One of the five senses

be impressed on the subconscious until it is felt, but once felt—be it good, bad or indifferent—it must be expressed. Feeling is the one and only medium through which ideas are conveyed to the subconscious.[1]

[1]Neville, FEELING IS THE SECRET, (Marina del Rey, Ca.: DeVorss & Co.).

Now I am getting more info. This is all making sense. It's all good.

Chapter IV

EVERY PERSON HAS
THE POWER OF CHOICE

Man's power of choice enables him to think like an angel or a devil, a king or a slave. Whatever he chooses, mind will create and manifest, wrote Frederick Bailes.[1]

so true

Yes, right within you at this very moment is this miraculous power of choice which will enable you to completely remake your world, your life, your affairs. You can stay right where you are, or you can move forward.

Reflection essay

There is no limit set by Infinite Mind. Man can go as far as he wishes, or stay where he is. His responsibility is to choose his destination: the only limiting factor is man himself. If he continues to sit and shiver in the cold, whimpering and complaining, that is his right as a free agent. But he can pick himself up and make his way to the warm glow of

man is his only enemy

[1]Frederick Bailes, *YOUR MIND CAN HEAL YOU*, (New York: Dodd Mead & Co., 1941).

51

the eternal fire, and enter into a life that contains all the elements of happiness. Others can help him but cannot do it for him; even God cannot do it for him. It is his job and his alone. On his voyage of self-discovery, he is the captain of his ship, and therefore solely responsible for making harbor.

Man's responsibility, then, is to choose his destination; the motive power to bring him there is furnished by the Infinite.[1]

Norman Vincent Peale had this to say about the power of choice:

The greatest power we have is the power of choice. It's an actual fact that if you've been moping in unhappiness you can choose to be joyous instead and, by effort, lift yourself into joy. If you tend to be fearful you can overcome that misery by choosing to have courage. Even in darkest grief you have a choice.

The whole trend and quality of anyone's life is determined in the long run by the choices that are made.

How to Choose a New Life for Yourself

Whether you realize it or not, you are now experiencing your past choices. Your tomorrow depends upon today's choices.

[1]*Ibid.*

Repetition (handwritten)

Choosing is the most important activity of your mind. When we learn to make clear choices easily and confidently, we begin to take dominion of our lives. Every choice is like facing a crossroad. Which road shall I take? Every decision is a choice.

Every time you make a choice you set in motion the Perfect Power of the universe for the purpose of causing your choice to become manifest in your experience. A choice becomes a direction to the individual subconscious mind which is one with the Infinite Subconscious Mind which Gustaf Stromberg called the Soul of the Universe. Herein lies the Power. The subconscious mind is like a willing servant, never asking you why, never questioning your choice, but carrying out the orders you give it with unerring precision. (handwritten: *just do*) *Choose what you really want, for you will surely get it. Choose your thoughts carefully for each thought is a seed planted in the creative medium of life.* (handwritten: *What about mistakes?*)

Only man has been given the power of conscious choice. Only man is co-creator with God. This privilege carries with it a certain responsibility. (handwritten: *Huge responsibility*)

You must make your own choices. Your very happiness depends on it. You are a unique individual. Your needs are known only to you. To let another make your choices can be disastrous. The Perfect Power within

(handwritten in left margin: *selected few*)

you knows what is right for you and will inspire you in making right choices.[1]

This is known as following your intuition.

A friend of mine has always had trouble making decisions. I know this because he has often tried to get me to make them for him. I was, therefore, greatly surprised to note a pronounced change in him. He now is confident and decisive. I could not resist asking him why this change. He laughingly said, "I've been reading your book on Self-Direction.[2] I have discovered that right within me lies the power to make choices!" He went on to tell me that he now receives his Guidance from the Teacher within when he asks for it. "You know, anyone can do this who is willing to trust the Teacher within," is the way he put it. "I ask and then I listen and Something tells me what to do."

You Must Make Your Own Choices

Beware of asking others to make your choices. Letting others make your choices is relinquishing your God-given freedom of choice.

You must start now to exercise your freedom of choice even if you make mistakes. It

[1] Jack and Cornelia Addington, *THE PERFECT POWER WITHIN YOU*, (Marina del Rey, Ca.: DeVorss & Co., 1973).

[2] Jack Addington, *PSYCHOGENESIS, Everything Begins in Mind*, (New York: Dodd, Mead & Co., 1971).

takes courage to be free. The more indepen-
dent choices you make, the stronger you will
become. If someone else makes your choice,
it is his inspiration, not yours, and some of
the power goes out of it for you.[1]

Your Choices Become Your Goals

Our day to day choices are very important because our choices shape our goals. Every choice is, in essence, a goal.

Therefore, when you have a desire, take a good look at it and ask yourself: "Is this really what I choose for myself?" If your desire is what you really want; if it is right for you; and if you can accept it for yourself, there is no reason why you should not have it.

How to Test Your Desires

There are four questions that you should ask yourself:

1. Does it exist?
2. Does it exist for me?
3. Is it right for me?
4. Can I accept it?

Can you honestly answer "yes" to each of these four questions? Then your desire is worthy of becoming your goal. *Does it exist?* Suppose your goal is for a large sum of money. You know that it

[1]Ibid.

Only if its right for you!

most people

exists. *Does it exist for me?* You can imagine it belonging to you. But, when it comes to question number three, perhaps you would feel guilty having this money. You might think that the only way for you to have this money would be to steal it or, in some legal way, take it away from someone else. You might worry that having such a sum of money might cause you to have more responsibility than you would care to have. Perhaps someone would want to marry you just for your wealth. If you can't answer question number three: *Is it right for me?* in the affirmative, stop right where you are. It is obvious that you won't be able to answer yes to: *Can I accept it?*

I know a fellow who is desperately in love with a girl. She exists all right, and she exists for him, but there is one obstacle in his way. She is married to his best friend. He feels that it would be morally wrong to try to take her away from her husband. At this point in time, his desire stops right there. Under the present circumstances, it would not make a successful goal.

And what about the young golf professional who desired above all else to become a tour champion. He spent a lot of money, time and effort attending the school provided for professional golf association tour members. He became qualified and joined the tour. He won a nice prize by finishing eighth in his second tournament. But, after three tournaments, he came to realize that he did not want to be a touring professional, after all. He discovered that he had a choice to make between the tour and his home and family. He saw that if he continued he would have to be away from home about 40 weeks out of each year. He made a choice at this point. He left the tour and accepted a teaching position instead. *Cool.*

As we ask ourselves the four questions, we must take into consideration that we are called upon to accept all of the responsibilities that go with our desire. There may sometimes be inconveniences. So, ask yourself, "In establishing my desire as a goal, am I willing to accept all of the responsibilities and inconveniences that may go along with it?" *good question*

Sometimes Our Choices Lead to Hard Work *Big deal !*

It would be nice to think our goals, once listed and placed in the treasure chest, would miraculously appear in due time without any effort on our part. This is not true. Life works through us, for us. We have to walk through the paces. Sometimes this involves hard work.

My wife and I have shared goals. One of them is to finish a book every year. We work together very harmoniously, but we work very hard. It takes weeks and months, and sometimes years, to finish a book. It all looks very easy when it's finished and

40 out of 52 ?

Hopefully he will pick family

ya right

It should be....' (handwritten margin note)

in print. The book once published, does not show how many times each page was rewritten, corrected, proofed for errors, typed and retyped. And this is just as well. The fact remains that it takes hundreds of hours of concentrated work to write a book. To us, the goal is worth the effort.

An athlete knows that to win he must practice his sport every day. During the last Olympic Games I thought, as I watched the swimmers slip through the water how many laps of the pool went before the finals—years and years of training.

> *It's the dream of victory and the willingness to make any sacrifice needed that builds Olympic champions, say three of America's 1976 gold-medal winners.*
>
> *"Find a dream, and then don't lose sight of it," declared 17-year-old Jennifer Chandler, who won a gold medal for springboard diving.*
>
> *"If you want to win, you've got to be prepared to give up the things you love, even if it means good-bye to your boyfriend. About two years ago I was going with this one boy. I liked him a lot. That was the problem. I wasn't paying enough attention to my diving. I knew that I had to make a choice."*
>
> *Jennifer chose to dedicate herself to a rigorous training program, often sacrificing slumber parties, dates and other joys of her teen years.*

Is all the sacrifice of an Olympic champion worth it?

"Yes, a thousand times over," says Matt Vogel, 19, who won his gold medal in the 100 meter butterfly swimming event. Vogel, who trained at least four hours a day months before the Olympics, exclaimed:

"If you want to make the Olympics, you have to be a dreamer. Have a long-range goal and work toward that goal, but don't lose sight of your sense of realism. Take one step at a time. This way you won't get frustrated quickly. A person can't expect just to jump into a pool and become an Olympic competitor overnight. Learn the basics, master them, then go on to the next step. You must be ready to give whatever it takes to get the job done."

Four years ago, after having to settle for a silver medal, he came to realize "that winners are people who understand themselves, who know what they respond to and want to achieve. The idea of succeeding kept me going. Athletes have to understand this. You have to have a dream," he explained, "then you must be prepared to push on to that dream." [1]

[1] Frank Zahour, *Three U.S. Champions Reveal Their Formula for Winning an Olympic Gold Medal*, (National Enquirer, September 14, 1976).

every last thing

The singer, the pianist, the dancer, the acrobat all know this. The prize is worth the effort. So, be sure to ask yourself: "Am I willing to 'take' everything that goes with my goal?"

Who Chooses Your Goals?
Who Is Your Secret Referent?

Are you choosing your own goals? Are they what you really want? If someone else is choosing your goals, if you are trying to please some friend or relative in the goals you select, you may not *want* to accept them and, of course, you will not attain them. Do it for yourself.

Many people are influenced subconsciously by some dominant personality, someone whom they desire to please, perhaps, or someone whose opinion is important to them. They examine everything they do, or think, or say, through this other person's eyes. This other personality becomes their secret referent. "Will my choice please girls ?" "Will girls approve of my goals?", etc. Children are apt to have secret referents in the desire to please parents or older brothers and sisters. Husbands and wives sometimes view everything through the other's eyes. Many emotionally immature people never get past the secret referent stage. It is important for all of us to examine our goals with this in mind: Are we choosing them for ourselves or to please someone else?

girls!!

Husband and wife partnerships, and other goal-oriented partnerships, can have common goals which are agreed upon. Such agreements are out in the open and are not cases of secret referents.

Sometimes Our Childish Desires Become Our Long-Range Goals

A child of ten may feel sure that he wants to be a doctor. Over and over he states: "I am going to be a doctor." If he believes this and does not change his goal, he will begin to identify himself with his objective and will begin receiving into consciousness thoughts in accord with this long-range goal. Everything he does will then contribute to that goal and he will eventually become a doctor. Fireman, va!l

Every little boy at some time or another wants to be a fireman or a policeman. Often this is a fantasy desire that does not become established in mind as a goal. But occasionally, such a fantasy desire becomes a goal that is deeply imbedded in the subconscious mind. In my graduating class in law school was a young chap who was outstanding in the class. To my great surprise, the day he graduated he told me that he had accepted a position as a patrolman on the Los Angeles Police force.

"Why in the world did you make such an effort to graduate from law school?" I asked him.

Do what you want.
What makes you happy.

"As long as I can remember, I've wanted to be a police officer," he told me. "I tried to put it out of my mind, but it was always there. Now I feel good. I'm finally going to do the thing I've always wanted to do."

Not only was he forsaking a possible legal career, but he left a job that paid him twice as much as he would get as a police officer. This made no difference. That long-range goal had been with him for a long time.

I love the comic strip, Benjy and Christopher. Benjy, a comical tramp, is sitting on a park bench talking to little Christopher who appears to come from a wealthy family.

"What do you want to be when you grow up, Christopher?"

"I don't know, Benjy."

"Well," says Benjy, "You ought to set goals and plan."

"Golly!" exclaims Christopher.

"Heck, when I was your age, I already KNEW I wanted to be a bum!"

Sometimes the Goal May Be to Stay Right Where We Are

Americans are so prone to think that things must continually be changing. More and more and more are the criteria. It is difficult for most of us to believe that a person could be contented doing what he is doing.

Johnny Mathis, the singer, had this to say about goals:

> *About five years ago, I stopped right in the middle of a thought, I was so startled by the realization that I really didn't have any goals. And it was O.K. It's still O.K. I don't want to do a Broadway show. I don't particularly want to do movies or anything like that. I decided what I really wanted to do was what I had been doing, and to keep trying to do it better. By the time I'm 45, when my voice will have reached its full maturity, I may know exactly what's going on up there on the stage.*

Johnny Mathis did have a goal. He is saying that he has the right to choose his own goals, not necessarily what other people might think his goals should be. To do what you like to do and to do it better is a worthwhile goal.

Negative Choices May Work Against You

Is it possible to make negative choices without realizing it? all the time!

Yes, indeed. Many people today are experiencing negative choices that they did not realize they had been entertaining subjectively.

Let's take a look at Job, that old Biblical character. Everything was going his way until, all of a sudden, his world collapsed. He lost everything—

family, wealth, children. He ended up sitting on an ash-heap scratching his boils with a piece of crockery. Pretty rough? What happened? Job answered this question himself when he said: *For the thing which I greatly feared is come upon me, and that which I was afraid of is come unto me.*[1]

Many people today draw to themselves accidents, losses, illnesses, failures and other undesirable situations because, through fear, they give undue attention to these things. The law is: *that to which you give your attention will become your experience.* This is the way the mind works in bringing the invisible into visible manifestation.

There are people who seem to attract one accident after another into their experience. Many times doctors label them accident-prone. Why do these so-called accident-prone people draw accidents to themselves? For various reasons. Some, to get attention and sympathy; others, because accidents are what they greatly fear. Their very preoccupation with accidents causes them to be in the right place at the right time to experience one. This is a prime example of how people entertain negative choices without consciously realizing that they are doing so. Then, there is the death-wish. Yes, believe it or not, there are those who have the wish to die, and they would be the last ones to admit it. Why? People wish to die for various reasons. Sometimes they are afraid of life. Some have a morbid preoccupation with death. Some

[1]Job 3:25

want to escape responsibility. Some just want to escape, period. This is a negative choice that the one entertaining it does not really understand. While we are looking at negative choices, let's not overlook the will to fail. There are those who have said so often, "I never succeed at anything I undertake," that eventually this becomes a pattern and they must fail to prove the statement. With some, it's easier to fail than to take on the responsibilities that go with success.

escape = death

The Subconscious Mind Can Be a Friend or an Enemy

Don't underestimate the power of the subconscious mind. But, neither should you fear it. If you recognize yourself in some of the foregoing examples do not allow yourself to feel trapped. The subconscious mind can be our greatest ally when we understand how to direct it.

Specify!

The man with vague and vagrant hopes
Is always hanging on the ropes,
Or vainly sparring with the air
Because he sees what isn't there.

He who would build a house must plan
The kind of house, the height, the span;
And know the stuff with which to build
If he would have his dream fulfilled.

And he must know down to the penny,
The size of nails, the kind, how many.
Do you want fir or oak or pine?
You'll have to lay it on the line.

This truth cuts sharper than a knife,
To build a home or build a life
There is one law you must apply—
Choose well your aim and **SPECIFY**!

Fenwicke L. Holmes

The book is getting
better and better.
I've learned the greates
power is the power of
choice.

       C. C.

Goals = Fun
(Game Plan)

Chapter V

GOAL-SETTING GIVES YOU A
GAME PLAN—MAKES LIFE FUN

Some people think that goal-setting is a dour and forbidding business. They don't expect to realize their goals anyway, so they are frustrated right from the start.

Goal-setting can be a lot of fun. It does not have to be grim at all. There is something about making a list that puts your goals into the creative process at once. It is like planting the seed. The goals are now planted in mind and all of life works together to help them grow.

list = creativity

Is It Necessary to Make Lists? *Yes*

Lists are important for several reasons. They help us solidify our ideas so that we will not try to go in two directions at once. They strengthen our desires and clarify our choices so that we are able to give concise orders to the subconscious mind. But, more than that, they are a marvelous way to measure our success and see how the principle of goal-setting works *for those who can believe in their goals, mentally accept them as already realized, and confidently expect them to come to pass.*

All of us have desires and dreams we long to experience. The ambition to succeed is built into us. Positive goals can be achieved. Keeping track of the goals that are achieved is a good plan because it builds confidence.

In the past, we may have felt that the years rolled around and nothing much was accomplished. Actually, we accomplished more than we thought we had, but having no way to measure our accomplishments, we were not aware of the gains we had made. Listing goals gives us a yardstick by which to measure our accomplishments.

There Are Many Kinds of Goals

When we speak of goals we are talking about a wide range of situations, circumstances, ideas and conditions. If one is to live a fulfilled, orderly, prosperous and happy life, one should set realistic goals and use the resources of the mind to achieve them. Whether or not you are at present in the habit of setting goals, there are things that you can learn about this highly necessary mental activity whereby you will be benefitted. Since much of our goal-setting is an automatic activity which is taking place without our even being aware of it, it is important to understand what we are doing and how to set goals effectively. Let's take a look at some of the different kinds of goals that go to make up our lives.

Long-Range Goals   Job; family

Many of our goals will be long-range goals. They may not materialize right away. My first book took thirteen years from the time it was conceived until the time it was published. Some seeds take longer to germinate than others; some goals take years before they become visible. Others spring up so fast we can hardly believe it.

We should not be quick to write off our long-range goals. Time is man's measure of eternity. Our long-range goals may be germinating beautifully in the invisible soil of the mind. Just because we cannot see them sprouting, we should not become discouraged and discard them. It takes patience to achieve long-range goals and, sometimes, a sense of humor. Also, it takes ingenuity to recognize the goal when it comes. A long-range goal is like a long journey; each step leads to the next. Sometimes there are detours. Still, each part of the trip is important and necessary to achieving the final results. Beware of becoming discouraged at some point along the way just because it does not look like the ultimate destination.

Tacking One Goal onto Another

I recently read in the newspaper the story of a man who achieved two long-range goals.[1]

"I am not sorry I gave up a big desk on Wall Street to come to San Diego and swing a hammer as a carpenter," says Steve Penner, 35.

"I am not sorry because I am doing one of only two things I ever have wanted to do." Penner does not point out that he is no ordinary carpenter. "The first thing I wanted to do was become a successful stockbroker in New York.

"So I left Houston, Tex., and went to New York and became one. I was vice president of a large, successful brokerage house on Wall Street when I quit to come to San Diego three years ago. I wanted a slower, different kind of life. I had been in San Diego in the Marine Corps."

Penner bought one old house in Pacific Beach and another in Coronado, and sold them restored for a handsome profit. Then he restored three others for San Diegans who had become his friends. "Actual restoration is expensive and it takes a lot of time," Penner said.

[1]Frank Rhoades, *The San Diego Union,* Friday, September 17, 1976.

[handwritten margin note: This is an example of an about face (total turn around)]

So the former stockbroker turned to building custom homes "to be sold to people who really care about the way they live." He spoke as if every nail was to be driven with loving care.

A goal

"I am building only two houses a year. That's all I'll ever want to build. I want luxury houses that will blend with the environment. This is my bag. It must be done because the environment here is so beautiful."

Penner's first custom house was built in La Jolla and sold for $165,000. He is finishing the second on Point Loma, and the price is $215,000.

"I have three carpenters who do things exactly as I want them done and I work right along with them," Penner said. "I learned carpentry by watching while restoring old houses."

total turn around

Many Long-Range Goals Are Compatible

Not all goals refer to careers. This story does not state how many other long-range goals Steve Penner might have had. Possibly he had a goal to learn a foreign language, or to play a good game of tennis. Or, find the right girl and have a happy marriage. You can have a number of goals at the same time as long as there is no conflict.

Hard to do

Linking Long-Range Goals to Achieve a Major Objective

Here is an example of how one can set into motion one set of goals in order to achieve another set of goals.

During World War II when I was in the insurance business I met a chap from England who had been disabled while serving in the British Army. Unable to go back into the service, Wade Harrison had affiliated with Lloyd's of London. They had offered him a brokerage firm in Mexico City, but first he had to qualify by learning to speak Spanish, as well as learning to organize and operate a large brokerage office. Equally important, he had to learn how to relate to Spanish-speaking people —their ways, their customs and their personalities. To accomplish these linking goals, he came to Los Angeles and affiliated with my company, the Victor Montgomery General Agency which had a connection with Lloyd's of London. His major goal-objective was to establish the brokerage office in Mexico City. His linking goals were the qualifying objectives given him by his firm. Wade began taking daily lessons in Spanish with a good teacher; every night he attended a Spanish-speaking movie with English sub-titles. He became friends with a number of Spanish-speaking families and was often entertained by them in their houses. He came to know the Mexican Consul and his family and made many favorable contacts that would help him in his new life. We admired Wade's diligence in learning all of the details involved in the functioning of a brokerage firm. Within a period of four months he was thoroughly qualified to assume leadership in his field and left for Mexico City to found a very successful brokerage firm for Lloyd's of London. This is a good example of linking goals to achieve a major goal-objective.

a lot of learning right there.

Sometimes Goal-Achievement Takes More Hard Work Than We Are Willing to Expend

Steve Penner was willing to work as a carpenter's helper in order to learn how to build and remodel a house. He worked hard and saw his hard work pay off when he was able to make a good profit on the old houses he restored.

My friend in the insurance business was willing to take what amounted to a crash course in insurance and Spanish. He worked in our office and spent every waking moment outside of office hours doing something to further his goals. There are many people who would not have been willing to invest the time and effort to achieve these goals. Many, lacking Wade's motivation, would have taken years longer to arrive at the ultimate goal. Everything has its price, especially our goals. So, with our long-range goals, we must ask ourselves: *"Are we willing to pay the price? Are we willing to*

That's for sure

Hard work = achievement

work and take the steps that present themselves along the way?" Yes

Short-Term Goals—Day-to-Day Goals—Clipboard Goals

We have seen that there are long-range goals that we expect to take years to accomplish, but what about the short-term goals that we expect to see ourselves achieving from week-to-week? The day-to-day goals and the hour-to-hour goals? Constant discipline is required with short-term goals.

I call my daily goals "clipboard goals" because I write them down on my clipboard and cross them off as they are accomplished. I find that once they are written down on the clipboard they have a way of getting done. If I just try to keep them alive in my head I am inclined to worry about them and they continue in the worrying stage for a long time. I advise anyone who would achieve a measure of order and efficiency to get the habit of making daily lists. Each day write down the six most important things to be done that day and then number them in the order of their importance. Start working on number one and continue on through the list. That is, do everything you can to further each goal. Your daily list may not be accomplished in one day and you may have to carry some of the goals over to the next day. Each day renumber them and give priority to your number one goal and continue down the list. Work on each goal in the order of its importance. Cross them off as accomplished. In this way number six may eventually become number one in importance but you will always be putting first things first.

I have just given you an idea that cost Charles M. Schwab, the great steel magnet, $25,000. He was talking to Ivy Lee and asked Ivy Lee if he had any new ideas. Ivy Lee told him about the clipboard and the six most important items for each day. Schwab introduced this to his staff. The next week he sent Ivy Lee a check for $25,000. This system could be worth $250,000 to you at today's inflated values.

Persistence Pays Off

As you work on your short-term goals, do not allow yourself to become distracted. We all have a tendency to avoid going ahead with a project. We get so used to making excuses for ourselves that we use them from force of habit to keep from working on our goals. "I don't have time"—"I'm too tired"—"I'll get to that some day." These are only a few of the excuses that our fertile minds cook up for us.

It is so easy to get caught up in a maze of outer distractions. If you have an interruption, and they will come, get back to your project as soon as possible. Persistence pays off. It is not necessary to struggle or push, just move quietly and confidently ahead doing whatever you can to accomplish your goal that day. Do not allow yourself to become annoyed or disturbed by interruptions, but analyze them to see if they are really necessary or merely a part of an old failure pattern. Eliminate unnecessary ones. Be flexible. Always be willing to adjust your goals if you find that you can improve them. Remember, procrastination comes from *pro,* meaning *forward,* plus *crastinus,* meaning *of tomorrow.* It means to put off until tomorrow what should be done today.

Combining Our Day-to-Day Objectives into Major Objectives

By the yard, life is hard,
By the inch, life's a cinch!

I don't know who said it first but it's surely true!

Our long-term goals are not going to drop out of the sky like meteors. They are going to require a lot of discipline on our part, a lot of work, generally. If you think you have to accomplish your long-term goals all at once you feel defeated. It was Laotze who said *a journey of a thousand miles begins with a single step.* It is the step-by-step, day-by-day activity that brings about the achievement of our long-range goals.

If your goal is to stop smoking, be a non-smoker

I know that word well (handwritten)

day-by-day. Alcoholics Anonymous advocates day-to-day sobriety. A step-by-step approach can be applied to overcoming any habit, or achieving any goal. Little by little, the goal will be achieved. Did you ever watch a woman crocheting an afghan, square by square, and then sewing them all together? Every day we watch the freeway being built, segment by segment. It seems that it will never be finished. And then, one day, it is all put together and the project is completed.

inch by inch not yard by yard

Moment-to-Moment Goals

Isn't setting moment-to-moment goals cutting it rather thin?

No, I think that moment-to-moment goals are the most important of all. If we can become master over the little things then we can become master over the greater things. If you can achieve moment-to-moment goals, then you are well on the way to becoming a consistent goal-achiever.

When you get into the car in the morning say to yourself, "I will drive carefully, within the law, and I will drive safely, to arrive at my destination at the right time." That is a series of moment-to-moment goals. *save lives*

Just before entering the office to keep your appointment, tell yourself, "I am going to be well received; I will accomplish my objective." It might be to make a sale. It might be to have your teeth cleaned. It might be to discuss a situation with your lawyer. Whatever it is, affirm a successful conclusion.

Now let's take another situation. Suppose you work in a factory. You travel by subway to your factory. As you leave the house, mentally say to yourself, "Today is a good day. I will travel safely to my work." As you arrive at your work, think to yourself, "Everything that I need to accomplish today will be accomplished with ease, with certainty, and in perfect harmony with those with whom I come into contact."

Suppose you are a student. As you walk into your school building you are thinking, "I am in harmony with everyone with whom I come in contact. I will do what needs to be done at the right time, in the right way. Whatever I need to know, I will know at the right time."

Does this give you a clue as to what we mean by moment-to-moment goals?

At first, you will be aware of having to make conscious decisions regarding goals. But after a few weeks of consciously directing your mind, you will continually expect everything to work out right; you will expect good to come to you, and people to react to you in right ways.

Goal-Setting Is for Everyone

Is goal-setting of value for everyone, or is it just for business people? Yes, everyone

Goal-setting has for so long been used by salesmen that it has become identified as a business

[handwritten in left margin: Don't say it out loud]

activity. This is far from true. Everyone can be benefitted by systematic goal-setting. Making a needlepoint is a goal; making a dress; cleaning the house; all the things that are done around a house are goals. This method of goal-setting works equally well for a business woman or a home-maker. It helps the busy person accomplish more with less effort and can be highly productive for a person who has very little to do.

Goals lists can open the way for more leisure time. The inclination is to spread a few chores out into many unnecessary hours. Suppose, for instance, a woman takes all day to clean up the house. She can change this pattern by setting time goals. Tightening up the time will make the work more interesting. The work, then, becomes a challenge, a game to be won. The end result is that more time is opened up for creative activities.

Goal-Setting Is Putting First Things First

Goal-setting is an orderly approach to right-living. It is not a materialistic approach. Goal-setting brings order into our lives and affairs. It is a method of putting first things first. Goal-setting makes sense. It brings direction into our lives.

If you want to go from San Francisco to New York, you don't toss a coin to see which direction you will go. You set out in the direction of New York with the goal in mind. Otherwise, you might wind up in Miami.

More loving... everyone should be

It makes no difference whether your goals are tangible or intangible. If your goal is to attain spiritual understanding, you can attain it, step-by-step. In the same way, you can become more understanding of others, more loving, even find happiness by setting goals for yourself.

Pain and Suffering Not Necessary in Attaining Goals

Not ... at all

Strange as it seems, there are people who are superstitious about setting goals as this excerpt from a letter written to me by a woman in New Jersey indicates:

> *I have the feeling that when I set down goals that will bring joy and a sense of achievement in my life, that to attain these goals means that I am going to have to have some kind of painful situation, such as an illness, or a financial loss, or the loss of a loved one. I had to tear up my goal list because I was afraid that I had to pay for the good things I was asking for by having something bad happen in my life.*

I feel this way sometimes

This letter shows a sense of unworthiness common to many people. This woman really does not feel worthy of accepting her good. Life does not play favorites. Anyone who plays by the rules can win the game. Possibly this woman has, in the past, experienced one of these negative situations which she has related to setting a goal. She needs to rid herself of this thought or it will continue to rule her life since that which she believes about herself is bound to become her experience.

Another mistaken idea that people have is that to succeed one has to push somebody else down, or take something away from someone else. This mistaken idea results in a feeling of guilt in regard to success. Possibly this woman has a guilt feeling about accepting her goals. Instead of condemning herself, she needs to affirm herself. She needs to know that she is important to life and worthy to receive her highest good.

There is also the old superstition that to be happy today means we will be unhappy tomorrow. Some people are afraid to be happy for fear their very happiness will invite misery into their experience. They have set it up in mind as a law that for every mountaintop experience they must go back into a deep valley. This is not true. It is possible to stay on an even keel and achieve one's goals without pain or suffering. *Cool.*

Keep Your Attention Focused on the Goal

Here's another letter that poses an interesting question:

I sit down and think about my goals until I get them rather clear in mind. A week later

I have forgotten what those goals were and realize that I now have other goals. Yet, I understand that the subconscious mind never forgets. What about this?

Your subconscious mind does not forget, but because of the changing scenes in your life, you are constantly changing your conscious responses. This is why I say that one should write out his major creative objectives and every now and then review them. You have to keep your eye single for life to work with you.

I was watching a football game on television. A player was just about to catch a pass when he took his eye off the ball to see if there were any tacklers near him. This seemed like a very logical thing to do but by taking his eye off the ball he failed to make the catch. That fraction of a second cost him and his team many yards.

Stepping Out on Faith
Not Stepping into Debt

I know people who spend their money before they get it and wind up deep in debt.

Emmet Fox used to tell a little story about a woman who heard him talk on building faith, after which she went to Wannamakers in New York and charged a lot of expensive clothes to her account. Eventually, Wannamakers began to press her for the payment of the bill. It was then she went to see Dr. Fox.

"But, I had faith. I stepped out on faith," she told him. No pe

"You didn't step out on faith," Dr. Fox told her. "You stepped out on Wannamakers!"

Misinterpretation happens to a lot of people. I am learning a lot and I have to remain posistive, have fun, and achieve.

Sound logical

Watch out
for failure

Chapter VI

NEGATIVE GOALS—
NEGATIVE RESULTS

Goals, goals, goals. Our lives are made up of goals. Did you know that your every waking thought establishes a goal? your every prayer? Even your decision to go to the market is a short-range goal. Goals are as natural as breathing. We are continually setting up goals for ourselves even though we may not be aware of it. The trouble is, many of these goals are haphazardly set, many are negative, undesirable goals. There is an old saying, *be careful what you ask for, you might get it!*

I receive many letters every day filled with negative goals that the writers have innocently turned over to the creative medium of mind. I am appalled at what these people are unwittingly ordering for themselves.

"I have been turned down on one job interview after another. I guess it's just my rotten luck," will result in more job turndowns.

"Every time I get a good job, it lasts just so long and then something happens and I get fired," is a negative order for more of the same. It amounts to having a negative goal. *Subconcious mind power*

"Why is it that my children don't love me and are so unkind to me?" is a subtle, negative goal that will keep the complaining parent in a martyred position.

Do you see what I mean? Do you see why it is so important to set affirmative goals and believe in them?

How Negative Attitudes Produce Negative Results

We have in our office a large addressing machine. Today, it works beautifully, but this was not always so. In the beginning, the young lady in charge of it was determined that it would not work for her. She called it "the monster" and expected the worst from it. Consequently, it was continually breaking down. All day long she was throwing up her hands in despair.

"It's the monster again!" she would exclaim with great feeling.

I used to chuckle when I heard her say, "If all else fails, read the manual!" She didn't read the manual, though, and we had one machine failure after another until she left. Then we hired a young lady to take her place who loved that old machine. Right from the start it worked beautifully for her, and has continued to run smoothly ever since. Negative goals can cause a lot of trouble. *Even if you don't know it.*

Negative attitude Negative results

When we understand the art of goal-setting, we
see why our goals have not always been met. It
opens up an entirely new concept of living. I have
come to the conclusion that goal-setting is one of
the most remarkable activities of mind. Once one
sets a goal, he opens the way for the Power to
come in and then all of life goes to work to see that
the goal is filled.

Goal-Setting Is an Art   A fine art

*Are you setting the kind of goals you really want
to see filled?*

Goal-setting is an art and a science. Goal-setting is based upon definite mental laws. Everyone
can use these laws. No one is counted out. When
you understand the scientific approach to goal-
setting, you will see why some of your goals have
been realized and others not. No one has an inside
track when it comes to realizing goals. *If you can
believe, all things are possible,* said the greatest
goal-setter of all time.

Why Some People Never Seem
to Realize Their Goals

In Chapter II, A FAR-REACHING EXPERI-
MENT IN GOAL-ACHIEVING, we told about
putting thousands of lists of goals in our "treasure
chest." Since that time, we have been receiving
letters from people in all walks of life, letters
concerning a great diversity of circumstances.

Letters from people whose goals are now being realized. But, now and then, there are those who say that none of their goals have been achieved. Why is this? There is usually a very good reason. *bad attitude*

In most cases where goals were not achieved it was because they were too vague. In many cases, the goals were of such a nature that anyone would have difficulty accepting them. In other words, they were not realistic goals. *Trouble*

Some of them were goals for others where it was obvious that criticism was implied; the goals were for the sole purpose of changing other people who apparently did not want to be changed. For example, mothers who wanted their sons to cut their hair, or to stop using marijuana. There were wives who wanted to change their husbands—husbands who apparently liked what they were doing. One of the great things we learned from this experiment is that everyone should set his own goals; that goal-setting and goal-achieving is an individual experience.

We should never attempt to foist goals upon another. It only leads to frustration on both sides. We can encourage another and lend him inspiration and ideas. *But we cannot set goals for another and expect him to achieve them unless he agrees wholeheartedly that the goal we have set for him is a goal he would have set for himself.* In other words, every goal must be individually tailored to the individual by that individual. Then the goal must become a mental reality within the consciousness of the one for whom it is tailored. It

Be specific

They should

Good advice ... to Parents

Cycle of life?

must become a "feeling thing" so that the one who will achieve it is able to feel that the goal is already accomplished in mind.

The Cycle of Achievement

In thinking about the wide variety of goals, it came to me that we should each consider a goal as being our individual creative objective. I use the word *creative* to emphasize that goal-setting and goal-achieving depend upon the creative medium that runs through all of life. It is personalized through the subconscious mind in each one of us. Therefore, the setting of right goals depends upon a creative acceptance within each one of us as to what is right for us. The achieving of the goal depends upon the creative expectation within each one of us. The cycle of achievement depends upon intuition from within; inspiration for ideas in setting the goal; imagination in visualizing it; and determination to persist until the goal is accomplished. It is truly an individual experience and that is why each one should set his own goals.

Do Not Expect All Goals to Be Achieved in One Calendar Year

I like to think of our long-range goals as *major creative objectives,* such as writing a certain book; graduating from college; having a family; starting a particular career; starting a business; buying and paying for a home; being released from prison (if a prisoner); accumulating a certain amount of money by a certain time; building a prosperous business, etc. There can be many creative objectives in a person's life because life has many facets. One can have creative objectives in business, creative objectives in mental expansion such as learning a new language or taking up some new study. One can have creative objectives in improving a family situation and in the spiritual realm. Your major creative objective can involve long periods of time if necessary. Do not expect all of your creative objectives to be realized in a calendar year. Everything necessary for its fulfillment may take years to unfold in its perfect sequence.

Often we have *minor creative objectives* that eventually turn out to be part of our major creative objectives, such as, passing all of the subjects in a semester of school; having a prosperous year in business; working out some problems concerning a teenage son; writing a chapter a week on a particular book; building a thought atmosphere of confidence and spiritual well-being; producing and putting on the market a certain product successfully; writing an article for a magazine, etc. We all have daily creative objectives which are very necessary to our day-to-day living program.

Negative Goals and a Positive Viewpoint

I have on my desk a letter from a woman who writes:

A long search has ended in a very exciting way. At last I took three pieces of paper and made the following lists:

1. *Things I do not want in my life.*
2. *Things I accept now.*
3. *Things I am thankful for.*

It surprised me to discover how different the whole picture became once it was on paper. Because the inspiration came from within, I can now express a desire I have had for so long. There is a strong conviction within me that there is a need for what I have and gladly give to life.

She then set down what was her major creative objective. By writing it down, she was able to identify with it and to clarify her thinking in regard to it. There is no question but that this goal will now be fulfilled.

Most People Are Too Vague in Their Goal-Setting

Now one of the things I have found through my correspondence is that most people are too vague in regard to goals and then they become discouraged when these vague goals are not met. Some make goals to be happy, or to be prosperous, etc. Such goals are obviously vague and uncertain of any measurement by which to tell whether or not they have been met. By the time the goal is

reassessed a new measure of happiness or prosperity is desired so that the goal-setter does not always
recognize his good when it comes.

New scale?

Goal-Setting Should Be Realistic

It is well to be specific in your goal even though
you do not outline how it shall come to pass.
There is a subtle difference here. The goal should
be something that you can imagine accepting,
something that is not beyond the realm of possibility *in your opinion*. For instance, for a person
who is having difficulty paying the rent for a one-
room apartment to set a goal of owning a 30-room
mansion is probably setting a goal that he would
find hard to accept all at once. We must all crawl
before we walk and walk before we run.

"Smokey" Gotta Crawl before ya walk.

own opinion is very important

Overcoming Adversity Through Positive Goals Can Bring Inner Strength

Elizabeth Dole, wife of Senator Robert Dole of
Kansas, while campaigning for her husband in the
1976 presidential election, visited Sharp Rehabili-
tation Center in San Diego, California. She had
asked to go there, although there were few votes to
be had in such a place, because she had a very
special interest in helping people overcome adver-
sity. She stopped at the bed of an 83-year-old
woman who had just had a stroke. She whispered

20 yrs later alls the same

to her, "You can do it, it really can be done. My father had two strokes in four years and he's still going to his office at age 83. Be a fighter. Really give it your all." And then she told this story:[1]

> "I know what determination can do and how much encouragement is needed," she said. "When Robert was injured in World War II, he was brought back from Italy with a broken neck, completely paralyzed from the waist down. His right arm was ruined. He underwent eight or nine operations in three years.
>
> "The turning point for him came when his doctor said, 'You can give up. Or you can accept it and grow up. Determine to have a recovery."
>
> Mrs. Dole told the reporter that she was convinced that adversity brought Dole an inner strength and character that enables him to cope with any situation now.

This is a clear-cut example of refusing to accept a negative goal and opting for a positive one. It would have been so easy for Senator Dole to have accepted the negative goal. He could have taken the easy course and allowed himself to be an invalid, cared for by the government, for the rest of his life. Those few well-chosen words of the

[1]Jeannette Branin, *The San Diego Union*, September 24, 1976.

doctor gave him the needed encouragement and he chose instead the goal of recovery.

Christopher Reed

Creating the Right Thought Atmosphere

Each one of us creates through his own thinking his own thought atmosphere. Ralph Waldo Emerson, the sage of Concord, said *a man is what he thinks about twenty-four hours a day.* A person's thought atmosphere is the sum total of what the person thinks about himself, his fellowman and his life experience. The reason that meditation is so successful is that in that quiet moment when one is totally immersed in the idea of God as Peace, Joy, Love and Beauty, he has entered into a conscious awareness of the Presence of Good in his life. For that little period, at least, he has let go of his erroneous thought atmosphere that was holding him back from his good.

One can entertain only one thought at a time. When we entertain a thought of love we cannot, simultaneously, entertain a thought of hate or fear. If we want to succeed in our goal-achieving it is important to create a positive, affirmative and loving thought atmosphere. Many people get into ruts of thinking negatively, destructively and unkindly about themselves and others. A negative thought atmosphere cancels out any progress that one may think he is making toward attaining his goal. Fortunately, changing the thought atmosphere is something we can do something about. As

Good is Good

negative thought = No progress

Paul said, *Be ye transformed by the renewing of your mind.* Not only can we do something about changing our thought atmosphere but our new, improved thought atmosphere becomes contageous, drawing to it all that is like it in substance.

The thing we have to keep remembering is that we alone are captains of our ship. We stand at the helm and direct it between the rocks, the shoals and the sandbars on a course that is right for us. Furthermore, the ultimate destination (the major creative objective) has to be selected by us. No one can select it for us.

Through our creative thought atmosphere we also let it be known what we expect from others in life. If we are expecting each person to be his best self, there is a strong possibility that that person will be his best self. This applies to our children, our partners in business, our fellow workers, and all people with whom we come in contact. We cannot set their goals but we can have good expectations for them, all of the time realizing that we have the ability to forgive them continually when they do not come up to our expectations.

Rule Out All Condemnation of Yourself and Others

Get judgment out of the way. How can you tell what is the proper time for a goal to be realized? Maybe it is already on the way and needs some other step in its sequence before it moves onto your horizon.

How do you know what is really best for others, what is necessary in their life experience for spiritual and mental growth?

Help, don't force.

Never accept defeat. If your goal is not met when you think it should be, forgive yourself for past mistakes and start over. Maybe the timing wasn't just right. Remember, God's time is the right time for all concerned. The Bible tells us:

> *To everything there is a season, and a time to every purpose under heaven; a time to be born and a time to die; a time to plant and a time to pluck up that which is planted; . . . a time to break down and a time to build up; . . . He hath made everything beautiful in his time.* (Ecc. 3. Read it all for it is beautiful.)

God is cool

Let your goals grow and unfold in God's perfect timing and you will never lack any good thing.

Prayer Is Goal-Setting

What about prayer goals? Aren't they a form of goal-setting? Yes

True scientific prayer is goal-setting in its highest form. The Master Teacher said, "It is done unto you as you believe," and, "What things soever ye desire, when ye pray, believe that ye receive them, and ye shall have them." He understood goals. Every miracle was a goal realized for all to see and marvel.

The Key to Goal-Setting and Achieving

What is the key to goal-setting and achieving?
That which you can conceive, in mind, believe, in mind, and confidently expect, in mind, will become your experience. You will note that I have repeated *in mind*. Everything takes place in the mind of the person setting the goal.

Is Defeat the End of the Game?

Can goals that are not realized cause one to feel defeated?
Yes, if one chooses to feel defeated.

There are many ways to react. One may ask "why?" and thereby gain a greater understanding of himself. Perhaps the goal was not what was basically wanted. Maybe the goal was not realistic or desirable. Perhaps there was not enough determination to achieve the goal.

The more one understands about goals, the less apt he is to be frustrated when goals are not met. Unmet goals can offer a challenge, with greater opportunities for growth and understanding.

Knowledge of Laws Helpful

An anonymous person who describes himself as "a very disillusioned goal-setter," wrote:

Just thought you might want to know that none of my goals are realized so far, NONE!!! And I had such faith before.

Did he? This person should re-examine the goals that were set. Something had to be amiss in the process of setting the goals or attaining them. What this person has said is like saying that the sun does not exist when it is behind a cloud.

Goal-setting and attaining is governed by laws that have always existed and always will exist. A knowledge, understanding and application of these laws will assure one of achieving goals. My feeling is that this person is determined to lose in order to prove that goal-setting does not work.

Tension and Goals

A man writes:

I don't believe in goals. They make me tense and I choke up. They are bad for me. Wouldn't it be better if I didn't have goals?

There are many people like this man. Because they are afraid they will not achieve their goals, they would rather fail at the very beginning rather than take a chance of failing in the process. This is a common failure pattern.

If you are one who has this pattern, you should definitely keep your goals a secret. Then, imagine what it would be like to fail in a goal. This takes the fear out of failure. You can see that failing is

[handwritten margin notes: "You must use the laws in the right manner." and "Have faith People"]

More advice

not so bad, but, if you had the choice, you would choose to succeed. Accept success as your goal and it will be your experience.

Goals Give Direction to Life

And then there is the person who sits under a tree and waits for life to happen!

Goals! I should say not! Trying to make a goal means you are trying to manipulate life. No, Sir! I don't use goals. I just let life happen.

Maybe

Setting a goal does not mean that we are manipulating life. Setting goals gives direction to life. If you don't have goals, you have no direction. You're going to drift and get nowhere.

When you go out in a sailboat, you do not always go with the wind. You select your objective and start sailing toward that objective. You may have to tack part of the way or all of the way. It makes no difference whether the wind is against you or behind you, you still use the wind to gain your objective. You set the sails and the wind does the work. You are not manipulating the wind but using it.

One ship drives East and another drives West,
  With the selfsame winds that blow,
 'Tis the set of the sails
  And not the gales
That tells them the way to go.

Like the winds of the sea are the winds of fate
  As we voyage along through life,
'Tis the set of the soul
  That decides its goal
And not the calm or the strife.

                              Ella Wheeler Wilcox

I am learning more and
more and hope these
techniques work for me.

Chapter VII

SOME USEFUL TECHNIQUES

Finally

Life is an individual experience. Each person is unique. Each person must think for himself. If you allow another to think for you he is cancelling you out. Each one must live his own life in his own way. No one can live your life for you.

Today we are faced with a maze of theory—theories about the economy, theories about environment, theories about child-raising, theories about self-development, theories about success. We are bombarded by theory through literature and the media. I propose to give you something more concrete, something you can adapt to fit your own life. I'm going to give you some definite, workable goal-achievement techniques that you can use. These are proven techniques that work *if you stick with them*. This is a work-book of practice and achievement. If you read it and don't put it into practice, it will, of course, be worthless to you. I'm counting on you to put it into practice.

and your existence

Finally

take some work

Some Workable Techniques You Can Use to Achieve Your Goals

1. The Technique of Choosing a Legitimate Goal
2. The Technique of Self-Identification
3. The Mirror Technique
4. The Technique of Visualization
5. The Technique of Treasure-Mapping
6. The Technique of Walking in the Dream
7. The Technique of Self-Determination
8. The Technique of Enthusiasm with Feeling
9. The Technique of Self-Direction
10. The Technique of Release
11. Good Leadership—Setting Goals for the Group
12. The Great Secret of Goal-Achievement: Using the Now Principle

The latter six are advanced techniques and will be dealt with separately in Chapter VIII.

Hope there is some explaination [handwritten]

How to Choose a Realistic Goal

Goals that do not conform to the laws of life are unrealistic goals that are not going to be realized. For instance, if I were to have as my goal, walking on the moon, and had no intention of becoming an astronaut, but relied solely on some handmade wings I had put together in my basement, I would have an unrealistic goal.

Duh, ya think- so ! [handwritten]

A person who has had a poverty consciousness all of his life and sets a goal to be a multimillionaire in a single bound is completely unrealistic.

The law is: *that which you can believe in, accept for yourself, and confidently expect, is bound to become your experience.*

A realistic goal is one that the goal-setter can believe in and accept for himself. If he can't believe it will happen, it won't. *have faith*

A realistic goal is a goal that is in accord with the laws of nature. I could say that my goal was to swim from Los Angeles to Hawaii, but my goal would be unrealistic.

I have recently taken up tennis after a lapse of many years. Would it be realistic for me to say that I could play on the Davis Cup Team or win the world championship? Since I could not accept either goal, they would not materialize for me. It has to be a goal that one can really believe in and accept for himself.

How a Seemingly Unrealistic Goal Can Turn Into a Realistic Goal

In 1948 Dr. Wernher von Braun, using a slide rule, worked out the calculations that proved the feasibility of an expedition to Mars. *What happened*

In a new preface to his classic on space travel, first published as a book in 1953, Wernher von Braun points out:

*'The logistic requirements for a large elabor-
ate expedition to Mars,' I said in the intro-
duction to the first edition, 'are no greater
than those for a minor military operation
extending over a limited theater of war.' I am
now ready to retract from this statement by
saying that on the basis of technological ad-
vancements available or in sight in the year
1962, a large expedition to Mars will be possible in fifteen or twenty years at a cost which
will be only a minute fraction of our yearly
national defense budget.*[1]

[handwritten: Destruction by man]

[handwritten: Well, we're here, but no Mars]

The rest is history. Dr. von Braun was right on
target, using his original computations, when, on
July 20, 1976, Viking I set down with a perfect
landing on Mars. *[handwritten: No man though]*

In 1954, Dr. Hans Friedrich who was Wernher
von Braun's associate, came, at my invitation, to a
meeting of a San Diego Men's Club and dia-
grammed the Mars Project on the blackboard. He
had no notes; it was all in his head. That night he
said that all they needed at that time was ten
million dollars to achieve the goal. Many of the
men who heard him that evening considered the
Mars Project an unrealistic goal.

[handwritten: That's all!]

And then, when man took his first step on the
moon, space travel was no longer just science

[1]Wernher von Braun, *The Mars Project,* University of
Illinois Press, 1953.

fiction. Today, as we all know, this once unrealistic goal has been realized using the original computations, proving again that that which we put into mind will become manifest.

Goals Must Be Something the Goal-Setter Can Accept

Coach Tommy Prothro of the San Diego Chargers was asked why he did not set a goal of winning all 14 games on the schedule. In a newspaper article entitled: *7 - 7 A REALISTIC GOAL FOR CHARGERS* he answered that question by pointing out that his players were mostly rookies, first year in professional football. He said that he wanted to build a strong team and this takes experience. Last year his team had won two and lost twelve. He was upping his goal this year. For the goal to be realistic, it had to be one that players could accept.

The Technique of Self-Identification

You've heard it said, *thoughts are things*. This is true. Everything was first a thought in mind. Whatever man can identify with in his mind is almost sure to become his experience. Therefore, when we identify with our goal and mentally live in the atmosphere of the attained goal, we are well on the way of achieving that goal.

When I started law school I took a course on legal orientation taught by Phil Gibson who later became the Chief Justice of the Supreme Court of the State of California. He told us in our first class that we should begin immediately acting like lawyers, thinking like lawyers and being lawyers. He informed us that we were not kidding ourselves, but everything we learned along the pathway would further substantiate this self-identification idea. It was remarkable how that whole class began to change their opinions of themselves and their attitudes toward each other.

The student who sets out to be a great surgeon, has to identify himself with this goal and move forward to finally attain it. This would come after he has completed all of the work necessary. I call this work the human footsteps that lead us from the known into the unknown. When it is accomplished, the goal is attained.

A person who sets a goal of selling a million dollars worth of real estate has to be able to accept such an accomplishment and feel himself actually accomplishing his great objective.

When the judges decided in favor of Muhammed Ali, Ken Norton was stunned. He, and a great many others, were sure he had won the bout. Norton has been accused of being bitter. Recently, he was quoted in the San Diego Union as saying:

> *If a person is to be good at what he's doing, he has to be motivated. Right now I don't*

Play the role

Success

an about face

Money is most People's reason for doing anything

have a goal. *The only reason to go on fighting is to make money.*

Motivation takes self-identification. Unless a person can identify with a goal, there is no motivation.

The Power of the "I Am"

The key to self-identification is that whatever you identify with the "I am," you become. "I am" is a state of being. It is up to us to choose what we will combine with our "I am." Will it be:

I am weak   *Opposites*   I am strong
I am poor   or   I am rich
I am unhealthy *attitudes*   I am healthy

Whatever we accept for ourselves becomes our experience. Therefore, if we do not like our experience it behooves us to change our self-identification. The supports of the self-identification technique are:

1. Change the belief about the self.
2. Believe in the new concept.
3. Accept a new image.
4. Live the new image.

Remember, it all begins in the mind. Gradually, what we involve, in mind, will evolve into the new experience.

Being Flexible Is Not Always Vacillating

I once had a roommate in college who wanted to be a doctor one day and a lawyer the next.

Since he was continually changing his objectives, he never did settle on any one career. Hence, he never attained a goal.

One day I addressed a service club on the subject of goal-achievement and was asked this question: *What about changing goals? Is this a sign of weakness? Should I charge on toward a goal that does not turn me on anymore?*

That's a good question. It *is* important to keep flexible. We all grow out of some of our thinking. We change within ourselves as time goes on and some of our old goals may no longer represent our deepest desires. Life is a chain of goals. Some we attain, others not. Some we outgrow before they come into being. When we attain a goal, we should set a new one.

Always keep stretching. The goals that made us stretch yesterday may need to be expanded today. It is still a matter of self-identification. What are you identifying with today? Every day we should be getting a little stronger in our beliefs, a little more confident, a little more assured. That is what goal-setting and goal-achieving are all about. That is why we at the Abundant Living Foundation have our Goals Program each year. It helps people develop self-identification.[1]

William James, who has been considered the father of modern psychology, declared that the

[1] If you would like to be a part of this program you may write ABUNDANT LIVING FOUNDATION, Box 100, San Diego, California 92138.

What sets us apart

greatest revolution in his generation was the discovery that human beings, by changing their inner attitudes, can change the outer aspects of their lives.

Man alone, of all the creatures on earth, can change his own pattern. Only man is the architect of his destiny.

The Mirror Technique

When you stand in front of the mirror what does the mirror tell you about your health, your psyche and your appearance?

Get a solution

If one looks in the mirror and sees that he is overweight, why not tell the person in the mirror that something should be done about it? Of course, that person in the mirror is *you!*

Self-direction, the science of directing your mind to achieve goals, really works when the process of self-identification is applied to it. If you look in the mirror and see that you are overweight, your tendency is to say to yourself, "I am fat," or, "I am 15 pounds overweight," or, "Do I really look like that?"

But, why identify with something you do not really want? Mentally, change the image in the mirror by changing that with which you identify. Even though you see an overweight figure in the mirror, think to yourself: "I am lithe, I am strong, I have a good body, I choose the ideal weight" (and name the weight that is right for you).

POSITIVE THINKING

As you look in the mirror, mentally change that picture and see yourself lithe, slender, just the figure you would like to have. Put your arms straight up and stand on your tip-toes and reach for the ceiling. The excess flesh seems to melt a bit as you reach. You can now begin to visualize the kind of body you would like to have. Identify with what you really want, accept it and then begin doing the things that need to be done to bring about the fulfillment of this desire.

The Technique of Visualization

When you go into an automobile showroom and evince some interest in one of the cars, the first thing the salesman does is invite you to get behind the wheel of that car. He encourages you to test-drive the automobile. He wants you to visualize yourself as the owner of that automobile. If he can do this, the sale is practically made.

Not everyone is able to think in pictures. Dr. Albert Einstein thought in equations. His wife said that every time he got an idea he wrote down an equation. His pockets were filled with old envelopes upon which he had written figures. A musician may think in terms of sound and harmony.

When it comes to goal-achieving, fortunate is the person who thinks in pictures for this brings abstract ideas into the realm of reality in the objective form. The technique of visualization is a very effective tool in attaining goals. One should

See it do it

Use it to your advantage

What if you're not visual.

Sub and Con Prevail again

visualize the desired result and then, after establishing a clear picture in mind, let go of all thought as to how the desired result will be attained. The subconscious mind begins to work on it and ideas come from the Source of inspiration deep within. These ideas are transmitted from the subconscious to the conscious mind. The conscious mind then takes the ideas that are presented and weighs them, and accepts that which appears to be the most acceptable method. The goal-achiever can then begin to move upon the goal, taking the necessary human footsteps. The whole mind works together to bring about the end result.

Visualization Is Not Just Daydreaming

Not a Goal

Visualization, to be considered a creative activity of the mind, has to have with it a desire to have that which is envisioned as fulfilled or attained. Daydreaming is a pleasurable thing and it is the activity of mind whereby a person fantasizes but does not intend to have any fulfillment of the fantasy. The creative imagination is brought into play in visualization. Albert Einstein said that imagination is more valuable than knowledge.

Visualization also includes self-image psychology. How does the person relate himself to the goal? Does he imagine himself attaining it or does he imagine himself unworthy? Does he think of himself as a person who has talents and ability, one who is able to see things through, or, does he envision himself as a failure, one who does not accomplish? Negative images can be reversed and changed. This is the beauty of mind at work. Nothing has to remain fixed. The only thing that is fixed and certain is the _perfect_ Power within which flows from an infinite Source and which is all-wise, all-intelligent, everywhere present, able to do all things. *Is any thing perfect in humans?*

Sometimes It Seems Like Magic

Sometimes visualization works so easily it seems like magic. A young mother with a little five-year old daughter to support was living in a poor neighborhood in very unattractive surroundings. Something must be done, she thought, about finding a better place to live. Housing was scarce and nobody wanted to rent to children, it seemed. She'd looked everywhere and, on the face of it, the prospect looked dismal. Then, her family invited her to come home for a visit and she put the matter out of her mind. Time enough to face the problem when she returned. Feeling lighter than she had for days, she decided to take the train and make the trip an adventure. As the train pulled out of the station, she laid her head back on the seat with a sigh. Nothing to worry about for three whole days!

And then she began to daydream. Without any

Negativity Stops Progress

Break result in good things

stress or worry, she pictured the kind of apartment she would really like to have. In her mind she saw it already: one story, bungalow type, just like a little house, used-brick with a planting box in front, brick fireplace, a little brick walk leading up to the inviting front door, a potted geranium on the front step. In her mind, she felt it was already hers. There was no longer any anxious longing, just a feeling of release and accomplishment.

In this mood she allowed herself to explore the interior of her dream home. It was just perfect! Knotty pine paneling on either side of the brick fireplace, even a plate rail for the antique plate collection! The master bedroom had a large walk-in closet and the little girl's bedroom was all that she had desired for her. The colors were right, everything made to order. She opened her eyes feeling happier than she had for days. It was just as if she had placed her order and could now forget about the whole business for the rest of the vacation. In fact, that was the last time she thought about the housing problem until they returned.

When they came home, the answer was clear. Their lives took an entirely different direction. She felt a strong urge to move to another city. Everything seemed to work together harmoniously and effortlessly now, where before life had seemed an uphill push. She told me later that it seemed as if she was being pulled along by an invisible hand,

Angel, God?

walking through the footsteps that led to the fulfillment of her goal.

When she got to the new city, she was drawn immediately to a certain area. It was as if she had been told to walk down a short street—a street that was only two blocks long. Neither she nor the friends who were helping her had ever heard of that street before.

And there it was! The dream house! It was used-brick with a planting wall and a red geranium in a pot on the doorstep! There were ruffled curtains in the window just like she had pictured them that day on the train. The little brick sidewalk seemed to beckon her right up to the door. The apartment was empty and obviously waiting for a new tenant. She went next door to inquire. At that moment a beautiful friendship began that lasted for years. The next door neighbor said that the apartment was available but the landlord had said "no children."

"However," she said, "when he sees *your* little girl, I'm sure he'll reconsider. Go see him. I'll call him and tell him you're coming."

It all worked out as if it were meant to be. The landlord *did* make an exception. A happy home was established for this young woman who dared to let herself dream of the kind of home she would really like to have for herself and her little daughter. Shortly after they moved in, she found the perfect right employment. And that, she said, was a bonus.

Woman's intuition

It will all work out

Some Goals Come Quickly Through Visualization

A woman needed a new sofa. She saw a picture in the newspaper that was just what she wanted. It was on sale, too, $100 off, marked down from $599 to $499. She tore the picture out of the paper and put it on her desk thinking she would go shopping before the sale ended. However, that week was filled to capacity and she never did get to the store that had advertised the sofa. But the subconscious mind had been working for her in the invisible realm of mind, drawing everything together for perfect right action. The following Sunday morning while reading the newspaper she did something she had never done before. She read the want ads under "furniture." She said at the time she wondered why she was doing it, it was so out of character. But all of a sudden she saw an ad that jumped out from the print as if it were begging her to read it. Here was a sofa advertised for sale. The ad said "like new." It sounded good. She went to see it. It was the exact sofa, the same brand, the same fabric, everything the same as the picture that lay on her desk. Only, this sofa which was practically new, was only $190. She had accepted a bargain and here it was, even better than she had asked for! The subconscious mind is not only our willing servant, but a miracle worker as well. When we learn to work with the subconscious mind we do not have to feel burdened. We learn to let the work be done for us through us. In the beginning God created the heavens and the earth. The heavens stand for the consciousness within, and the earth is the outer experience. That which we can accept, in mind, is already on the way to becoming our experience.

The Technique of Treasure-Mapping ?

Treasure-mapping is a way to visualize your goals, a very effective way. Some years ago a magazine called The Nautilus ran a contest for the best article showing how a treasure map had helped to bring about someone's heart's desire. The competition attracted nationwide interest. During the contest many found that treasure-mapping really worked. *so yrs. later the same*

It was in the winter of 1946 that I first became interested in treasure-mapping. The first treasure map I ever saw was made at my house on a rainy New Year's Day.

We were living in Pasadena on the rim of the arroyo overlooking the Rose Bowl. We had four tickets for the Rose Bowl game and had invited another couple. Our plan was to have lunch at our home and walk down to the Rose Bowl.

It was one of those rainy New Year's days. It rained all day long! Bill and Mary arrived around noon. We had a big fire in the fireplace and ate our lunch in front of the fire. Because of the constant downpour and the inviting fireplace fire, we just didn't go to the game.

Find the technique that'll work for me

Our guests were in the process of making some changes. Bill was in the insurance business, selling as an independent agent. In the course of the afternoon, he explained that he really would like to be working for a big agency, in charge of the group health and accident department. I suggested that he write it down and consider it a goal. I suggested also, that he visit such an agency, and walk through the place to get the feel of it, what it would be like to be in such an organization. We spent about an hour talking about what it would mean if he had such a position.

He began to visualize himself traveling throughout the country, setting up these group plans in various large organizations. The more he talked about it, the more enthusiastic he became about the idea. *He was doing it*

He talked it over with his wife, and she, too, was enthusiastic about his doing this. His idea seemed to begin to materialize as we talked about it.

On that same afternoon, Mary started her treasure map. We found a large piece of white paper and Mary worked all afternoon, cutting pictures out of magazines, pictures of the kind of a house they would like, the furniture, etc. Mary even planned for the number of children she wanted and pasted pictures of children on her treasure map. They found a picture of a man sitting at a desk in a beautiful office and wrote "Bill" above it, adding the words, "In charge of a large group health and accident department."

Visualize

See it, feel it, do it!

It's grain

Shortly after this, Bill made application with a firm that had a nationwide health and accident group plan. The person who took his application told him that he had heard of a nationwide firm that had never entered the health and accident group market. Bill immediately made an appointment to see the local manager of this big firm. He explained his idea to him, how their existing clients could all be contacted and solicited for group health and accident insurance.

The local manager happened to be the son of the President. He immediately called his father and got his consent to establish this new department, and let our friend go ahead developing it.

This was 30 years ago. Two years ago Bill retired as Vice President in charge of group insurance. In the meantime, he had built a department that insured many of the largest corporations in the country.

Recently Bill and I were talking about this and he said that it was quite remarkable that when he first entertained the idea in front of the fire in my living room, that rainy New Year's Day, it was an idle dream. He said that had he not written down what he really wanted, and identified with it, he would never have done anything about it. But, the real clincher, he said, was the treasure map. It brought everything into focus.

When a goal is established in mind, the human footsteps to bring it about will follow.

Treasure-mapping can be done for any goal,

tangible or intangible. It enables one to more easily visualize the things that he would like to have come into his experience. I have known people to find the very house design pasted on the treasure map. It works equally well in finding a certain type of automobile, items for a collection, antiques, almost anything one can imagine.

If the desire is for something intangible, such as a college education, pictures can suggest a university campus where the treasure mapper can visualize himself, or herself, completing his studies. If the desire is to become recognized in a profession, one could cut out a picture of a doctor, or, if the desire is to be a lawyer or a judge, cut out a picture of a courtroom with lawyers and judge at work there. If the desire is for inspiration and a high spiritual consciousness, uplifting scenes might be used, such as snow-capped mountains or cloud effects, anything that lifts the soul.

The idea is to bring enthusiasm and visualization into living by making a game of goal-achievement. Treasure-mapping is a good way to do this.

Make it fun

The Technique of Walking in the Dream

If you can mentally possess your goal and feel yourself in the midst of it, you have taken a long step toward achieving it. When Abraham and Lot decided to go their separate ways, the Lord said to Abraham:

If you see your goal in front of you the desire becomes greater.

Lift up now thine eyes, and look from the place where thou art northward, and southward, and eastward, and westward; for all the land which thou seest, to thee will I give it. . . . Arise, walk through the land in the length of it and in the breadth of it; for I will give it unto thee. (Ge. 13:14, 15, 17, 18)

This is what is needed. We must walk through the land of our dreams until we can possess the land in mind.

This is exactly what a young woman in search of employment did recently. She wrote me the following letter which I thought was a wonderful example of the technique of walking in the dream:

Rejoice with me! I begin my right and perfect employment tomorrow, an amazing demonstration!

On Wednesday of last week I was interviewed for this position. I was told they would let me know on Friday. The position requires I be at work at 7:00 a.m., so for three mornings I arose at 4:45 and at 6:40 I would leave the house, drive to the office and imagine that I would unlock the door, turn on the lights, make the coffee (a duty of the position), empty the wastebaskets, etc. When I arrived back home I would begin typing as though I had typing to do first thing. On Sunday morning I pretended I had an assignment to take some photos (that, too, will be part of my work). With such an assignment in mind, I took some photos of a building I had long wanted to photograph.

The only other person to whom I mentioned my position was a friend who would understand. I must say, that by Saturday at midday I had the feeling that the decision had been made in my favor. I could imagine myself really filling that position.

This morning, I "went to work again" as I had been doing. At 8:30 a.m. as I was thinking of informing my friends as soon as I knew I was accepted, the phone rang. It was Mr. P., asking me when I wanted to start work! I told him tomorrow. It is all set. This is the greatest day of the year!

Yes, she got the job and this was just the beginning for it heralded a whole series of goals realized in her experience.

Be Careful Where You Walk— Some Dreams Are Nightmares

It becomes very important that we become discriminatory in what we ask of life because the ideas that we entertain in mind are very apt to become our experience.

Did you ever imagine yourself telling the boss off? And then found yourself doing it when you wished you hadn't? Did you ever become irked over some fancied injury and imagine yourself getting even with the other person, planning long conversations in the dark of the night? When it finally materialized, it turned out to be just the wrong thing to do. It has been said, "the subconscious mind has no sense of humor." It assumed you wanted it that way.

Many accidents are the result of fearfully picturing again and again some dire circumstance. What is greatly feared will come to pass. Poor beleagured Job said, "For the thing which I greatly feared is come upon me, and that which I was afraid of is come unto me." It is well to ask ourselves when we start imagining something in the future, "Is this something that I really want to experience?"

an unquestioning Servant

Repiton

I am learning more an more and other people's stories of success are exciting to hear

Chapter VIII

ADVANCED GOAL ACHIEVEMENT
TECHNIQUES

The Technique of Self-Determination

Self-determination is defined by Webster as *determination of one's acts by oneself without external compulsion.* The technique of self-determination is the art of not being influenced by others. It involves seeing our goals being attained without relying on others to give us encouragement. Through self-determination we take dominion over our lives and affairs. It is having the courage of one's convictions.

The Place of Willpower
in Goal-Achievement

How does willpower fit into the idea of goal-achievement?

Willpower and self-determination go hand-in-hand in attaining goals. By this, I do not mean that we are to force our will upon life. We use the will to keep the attention on the goal. Force has a tendency to push the goal away, but quiet perseverence in keeping the attention focused on the goal, as though already attained in mind, is the real key. In the mind's eye, we think of the desired result. We accept it as a part of our new experience in life. We feel ourselves living in this desired result. In this way, the impression is made on the subconscious mind. As we persist in thinking about our goal, we think of it not as a far-off dream but as being already accomplished. We protect it from doubt, fear and anxiety, or any other negative thoughts until it has become manifest in our experience.

This is the role of self-determination: perseverence, persistence and focusing the attention. This is the way we use willpower effectively.

Think of the goal as accomplished (handwritten)

Don't Quit

The Key to success (handwritten)

When things go wrong, as they sometimes will,
When the road you're trudging seems all up hill,
When the funds are low and the debts are high,
And you want to smile, but you have to sigh,
When care is pressing you down a bit,
Rest, if you must—but don't you quit.

Life is queer with its twists and turns,
As everyone of us sometimes learns,
And many a failure turns about
When he might have won had he stuck it out;

Be Determined (handwritten)

Don't give up, though the pace seems slow —
You might succeed with another blow.

Often, the goal is nearer than
It seems to a faint and faltering man,
Often, the struggler has given up
When he might have captured the victor's cup,
And he learned too late; when the night slipped
    down
How close he was to the golden crown.

Success is failure turned inside out —
The silver tint of the clouds of doubt —
And you never can tell how close you are,
It may be near when it seems afar;
So stick to the fight when you're hardest hit —
It's when things seem worst that you mustn't quit.
            —Author unknown

Centering In, or the Value of Concentration

You can see why it is so important to have a target. Many people never realize their goals because they have never decided what it is they would like to achieve. They take whatever comes along without setting up any objectives. It is not just a matter of wishing but of concentrating the attention on reaching the goal. It takes discipline and persistence. Anyone can achieve his aim in life if he is prepared to pay the price.

Be All you can Be

No pain no gain.
(payment)

The Technique of Enthusiasm with Feeling

Ralph Waldo Emerson once said, "Nothing great was ever accomplished without enthusiasm."

Everyone has a direct line to an infinite Source of Power. Enthusiasm turns on the switch that connects us to that Power. The word enthusiasm means divine inspiration. Its root words are *en theos* (in God).

Many a person has lost his goal when he lost his enthusiasm for it. Enthusiasm is an inward feeling of being empowered by Life Itself. There is no accomplishment without it. When one loses his enthusiasm he starts deteriorating mentally and physically. It's the quality of feeling that one invests in his desire that determines how far it will go toward being realized. In order to achieve any goal one must maintain enthusiasm with feeling. Optimism is the expectation of good. Coupled with enthusiasm, it guarantees the accomplishment of any goal.

Did you ever have an idea that seemed terrific at the time, perhaps it was for a labor-saving invention, or a new business, something that would help mankind. For about a week you were all "revved up" about it. And then, you thought about all the work that was involved, the years of effort it would take to put it all across. Something went out of the dream. Your enthusiasm. After awhile, you forgot all about it. When you lost your enthusiasm, you lost the power to motivate your idea and it fizzled. The goal became still-born. It died in the embryonic stage.

Every successful enterprise starts with a dream which is empowered with enthusiasm. The trick is to keep the enthusiasm from leaking out. Recently I attended a meeting in a large hotel ballroom. Four thousand people were there. Tied to each chair was a helium-filled balloon. It was a dramatic and colorful sight, four thousand balloons rising toward the ceiling. The plan was to take them outside into the plaza of the hotel on the following morning and release them *en masse* to soar into the blue and float over the city of Chicago. What a dramatic show they would make! We could hardly wait for the next day. But, when we came to the morning meeting we were met with a dismal sight. The helium had partly leaked out of the balloons. They had lost their enthusiasm.

Joseph M. Segel is a man with enthusiasm. In 1964 he conceived the idea of establishing The Franklin Mint for commemorative coins and medals. His was a new idea and he encountered many challenges, many obstacles, but his enthusiasm for the idea carried him forward and encouraged all those around him. Today The Franklin Mint is highly successful and this success is primarily due to the enthusiasm and vision of this man. His ability to achieve his goals is due to the fact that he not only did not lose his enthusiasm but shared it with everyone around him. Recently he said:

What really makes The Franklin Mint successful is its philosophy. We don't look around for old ideas. We concentrate on creating new ones. We don't look backwards. We look ahead to a vigorous and exciting future that will involve everyone associated with The Franklin Mint—sculptors, engravers, press operators, packagers, engineers, and collectors. It's people who give The Franklin Mint its special strength.

Not long ago I was having lunch at a coffee shop where the tables were rather close together. Two men were at the next table and I couldn't help overhearing their conversation. One was happy, healthy, affirmative about everything. You could tell he loved his life. There were laughter wrinkles at the corners of his eyes. He was filled with exuberance. He was talking about his work as a teacher. His class, it seemed, was very enthusiastic about the program and so was he. It came out that he had two part-time jobs, custodial work, but he didn't feel the least bit burdened. He said it was O.K. He didn't mind it. Really easy. Everything was good. He was relaxed and thoroughly enjoyed life. It made me feel good just to look at him.

The other man resisted life right down the line. He couldn't get a job; there was something wrong with every job that had been offered to him. He was the most nervous man I have ever seen. He

[margin note: Enthusiasm = success]

[margin note: Still going strong today]

[margin note: enthusiasm = happiness]

[margin note: Nerves = Depression]

had a tic; his face kept twitching as he talked. He was thin, cadaverous, almost a caricature of his type. *Missed the train*

I couldn't help thinking, the first man was letting the divine potential live through him. He was investing himself in life. He was young, enthusiastic, and you knew he'd go a long way. The other man was afraid of life and that's why he was so critical. Because he was afraid of failure, afraid of getting criticized, he thought that life was against him. And so he was bottling up his divine potential. I longed to tell him that all he needed to turn his life around was a change of attitude, a little enthusiasm and a goal he could believe in.

The Technique of Self-Direction

There is only one point where we can take dominion of our lives and that is at our point of use of the conscious mind.

It is the conscious mind that does the directing. Here we choose the kind of thoughts that will provide the mold for the kind of experience that we would like.[1]

You are the center. It all fans out from you. You choose the direction you will take. It all takes place in thought, your thought. You choose your direction. It can be toward achievement or failure. It is up to you. All this is an inner experience

[1]Jack Ensign Addington, *PSYCHOGENESIS*.

that may not, at first, seem very important to you; but once you see what a great effect self-direction has upon your outer experience, you will have great respect for this technique.

> *You alone give the orders to your subconscious mind. Maybe you think you are in bondage to what someone else thinks about you, and accepts for you, but it is only because you have accepted this for yourself. Change the belief and you will change your experience. The most important thing that you can learn in this life is that you alone choose your thought and your thoughts shape your world.* (Addington, *Psychogenesis*)

How Negative Self-Direction Defeats One

"Most people are victims of self-fulfilling prophecies," writes Ronald Kotulak in a front page article in the Chicago Tribune. He goes on to say, "If you've ever said to yourself that there was something you couldn't do, or that you knew you'd fail, or that there was no use trying, then probably you were making your own prophecy of failure come true."

To back his premise he quotes Thomas Dolgoff who teaches mental health administration at the Menninger School of Psychiatry, Topeka, Kansas: "The theory of the self-fulfilling prophecy holds that people tend to do what is expected of them and that even a false expectation can evoke behavior that makes it seem true. Our belief that something will happen can actually make it happen."

Self-Direction Worked for Her

For twenty years she had dreamed about taking a vacation trip to Hawaii. How many times we had all dreamed of such trips but made no move toward the goal. We gave ourselves many reasons why it could not happen—too expensive, don't have time, can't leave home or office, etc. We dared not believe such a goal was for us.

Recently a woman who decided to try my system of goal-setting and goal-achievement wrote to me:

> For at least twenty years I have dreamed and desired so much to be able to take a vacation trip to Hawaii but have never been able to do so. Last week I wrote down this goal, expressing thanks for it. Last night, just one week later, my employers told me that our company had won a trip to Hawaii in January, for eight days, all expenses paid and they wanted ME to go.
>
> I have worked in dealerships for the past twenty-five years and have seen many, many trips won from the manufacturers, but NEVER have I ever known a dealer to offer one to a female office manager. This is indeed God's answer to my dream and desire. I am so very,

very grateful! My entire life has changed since I found Abundant Living and changed my way of thinking.

For twenty years Vera had believed that it was not possible for her to go to Hawaii, but when she wrote her goal down she solidified it. It now had direction—self-direction. When she gave thanks for the trip, she accepted it in her own mind and now nothing stood in the way of the fulfillment of her goal.

If you think you are beaten, you are;
    If you think you dare not, you don't.
If you'd like to win, but think you can't
    It's almost a cinch you won't.
If you think you'll lose, you're lost,
    For out in the world we find
Success begins with a fellow's will;
    It's all in the state of mind.

If you think you're outclassed, you are;
    You've got to think high to rise.
You've got to be sure of yourself before
    You can ever win a prize.
Life's battles don't always go
    To the stronger or faster man;
But soon or late the man who wins
    Is the one who thinks he can.

Walter D. Wintle

Attitude is everything
Be happy, Don't Worry

Jerry McGuire

Good Leadership—Setting Goals for the Group

A leader is a person who is going some-where—but not going alone, said Walter MacPeek. *He takes others with him. His skill lies in setting up situations in which other people are willing to follow him and are happy to work with him, a precious skill called leadership. This skill is made up of many qualities—thoughtfulness and consideration for others, enthusiasm, the ability to share responsibility with others, and a multitude of other traits. But fundamentally a leader is one who leads, one who has a plan,* **one who keeps headed toward a goal and a purpose.** *He has the enthusiasm to keep moving forward in such a way that others gladly go with him.*

The mark of every good leader is the persuasive ability to draw a group together and motivate them into pursuing one common goal.

Making Your Goals Their Goals

I am going to let Robert Levinson, an outstanding business executive, give you some words of wisdom on this subject:

However bright you may be, as every savvy manager knows, you will find it immensely difficult to make any truly significant career-

building headway without the whole-hearted cooperation and support of your people. Here's the way Sam Johnson put it almost two centuries ago: "No degree of knowledge attainable by man is able to set him above the need of hourly assistance." It's just as true today.

You can't go it alone. You're going to need help. The trick is to spur your people to adopt your goals as their very own, and to drive toward their fulfillment with the same vigor and zest that you yourself apply.

Do this and you will capture the very essence of management savvy.

Here's an interesting thought. The car you drive and the people you supervise have a great deal in common. Sound crazy? It's not. In a very real sense the people who work for you are your transportation. **You can depend on them to get you where you want to go in your company and in your field,** just as you depend on your car to get you from one place to another.

Now let's expand on our parallel. For a car to travel smoothly, without stalling, without breaking down, you keep it maintained and in good repair, well oiled, properly fueled. Same thing with your people. You maintain them with training, oil them with information and guidance, fuel them with the kind of motivation that will inspire them to do what *you want them to do in the way you would like them to do it.*

SHOOT FOR THE SAME TARGET

Arthur Sulzberger once wrote: "They said of Queen Victoria that she never looked to see where the chair was before she seated herself. She **knew** *it would be in its proper place. On a team there is no substitute for confidence in one's teammates."*

On the management team especially. The skilled, savvy manager is an expert "confidence man." He sharply defines profit goals. He sees to it that his people all shoot for the same target.

In short, what the savvy manager scouts for are business skills and business instincts that complement—and compliment—his own.

NO CARBON COPIES

Caution. Don't interpret "complementary thinking" to mean carbon copy or "yes man" response from your people. What the truly savvy manager wants is goal agreement, not methods agreement.[1]

Why Some Group Goals Are Never Achieved

A veteran member of the San Diego Union staff recently recalled that he had written an

[1]Robert Levinson, *Spur People to Make Your Goals Their Goals,* Sky magazine, June 1976.

extensive article about alternatives to Lindbergh
Field, the present San Diego airport. It was published on the day of his son's birth. His son now is a
Junior in college. San Diego is a good example of
where there has never been a common agreement
on a group goal — the goal of finding, locating and
building a proper airport for the city. The city
needs a new airport. Everyone agrees on this. The
present airport is too small and is located in the
heart of the city. Large jets cannot come into this
airport and there is no room for expansion. Many
possible locations have been proposed. Several are
adequate in every way. Yet, the Board of Super-
visors cannot agree on a location. Not one of them
wants the airport in his district. Every property
owner agrees that the new airport is badly needed
but no one wants it near his property.

A group is composed of individuals, individuals
often moving in different directions. This is why it
is so hard to get things accomplished where
politics is concerned. There must be common
agreement before any goal can be achieved. It
takes good leadership to persuade a group that
they want a common goal.

Sometimes a war seems to serve as a motivating
tool in drawing a group together. Take England.
During World War II goals were achieved in a
miraculous way through the leadership of Win-
ston Churchill.

The United States in both World War I and
World War II had a common enemy and a common goal. We were victorious. The Vietnam War

became a fiasco because we had no common goal of victory.

It is not enough for a group to give lip service to a common goal, there must be a real will to win drawing them all together. It takes a strong leader and a willingness to follow that leader. As Ayn Rand once said, "A board of directors is the shadow of the strongest man on the board."

Every leader learns sooner or later that you cannot set goals for other people and expect them to work with you, but you can get people to share in your goals and cooperate with you in their achievement.

The Great Secret of Goal-Achievement, Using the Now Principle

The reason many people fail to achieve their goals is that they think of them in the future tense —tomorrow I'll make those telephone calls; next year I'll make my quota; ten years from now I'll be on easy street. Tomorrow never comes. Next year is always a year away. The goal is always the carrot on the stick in front of the donkey. The faster you run the faster it moves ahead of you. This is why I say to you: THE GREAT SECRET IS USING THE NOW PRINCIPLE.

The "now principle" in goal-setting refers to using the present tense in setting the goal. The goal must be accepted in mind NOW, not tomor-

row or some future time. There is a time for
sowing and a time for reaping. There is a time for
setting goals and a time for the goals to materialize. There is a time for working and a time for
resting. There is a right time for everything to
come into our experience and we prepare the way
by thinking in the *now*.

Thinking in the *now* telescopes time and often
brings the end result much sooner. Vera, whom I
mentioned earlier, had her twenty year dream of
going to Hawaii materialize in a week, a good
example of what can happen when one accepts the
goal-achievement *now*.

Jesus was a great one to think in the *now*. It is
said that the Aramaic language (the language of
Jesus) was all in the present tense. The Lord's
Prayer was given in the present tense. And Jesus
told his followers, "What things soever ye desire,
when ye pray, believe that ye receive them and ye
shall have them." This means to set the goal and
then create the image of receiving it. And, at the
right time, it will come into your experience. This
explains why our little, almost inconsequential
goals, come so easily. We do not set up the same
barriers of unbelief for ourselves.

If your goal is to move into a new home, do not
move out of your old house and live on the curb,
but start visualizing yourself living in your new,
ideal surroundings. You'll be surprised how fast it
will all work together for you to achieve your goal.

If your goal is to earn money, do not rush out

and spend what you do not now have, but visualize yourself having the money in your possession. See it in your bank book. See yourself paying the bills.

Every year, at our Foundation, we have what we call the "Unexpected Money Program." People work on opening their minds to receive their supply in unexpected ways. And they do. The many letters I receive prove it. Ideas come that they had never anticipated. The results have seemed fantastic to me—paintings sell, stories sell, unexpected legacies seem to come from nowhere. It is all a matter of opening the mind to receive in the NOW.

Every goal must be accepted, in mind, as already accomplished before it can appear in the outer.

Dr. Maxwell Maltz wrote in PSYCHO-CYBERNETICS:

> *Your built-in success mechanism must have a goal or target. This goal, or target, must be conceived of as "already in existence now" either in actual or potential form. It operates by either (1) steering you to a goal already in existence, or by (2) discovering something already in existence.*
>
> *The automatic mechanism is teleological, that is, operates, or must be oriented to "end results," goals. Do not be discouraged because the "means whereby" may not be apparent. It is the function of the automatic*

mechanism to supply the "means whereby"
when you supply the goal. Think in terms of
the "end result," and the "means whereby"
will often take care of themselves.[1]

[1]Maxwell Maltz, M.D., *Psycho-Cybernetics*, (Englewood
Cliffs, New Jersey, Prentice-Hall, Inc., 1960).

I have learned many
new techniques and every-
thing is coming together.
I love it.

Chapter IX

CREATIVE IMAGINATION—
THE MIRACLE WORKER

How William Blake must have shocked people when he spoke of imagination as if it were divine! He said:

> *I rest not from my great task to open the eternal worlds, to open the immortal eyes of man inward into the worlds of thought: into eternity ever expanding in the bosom of God, the human imagination.*

This is indeed a different approach to divinity, but is surely one that deserves some attention as it opens up a whole new field of human progress. It is through creative imagination that man has moved from the known to the unknown, and will continue to do so. The greatest painting has never been painted; the greatest literature has not been written; the finest music has not yet been composed; the greatest invention has not yet been perfected. It is through creative imagination that we reach out into expanding consciousness with ideas to conquer the unseen worlds of science, knowledge, culture and human and spiritual understanding. Creative imagination goes before us to point the way.

Creative imagination is one of the most dramatic tools that life has given us. It is the means by which God creates through man. William Blake understood this so clearly, and even though he was penniless, he created works of art through his painting and his words that are now priceless and beyond compare. Since each person is unique, his use of creative imagination is not comparable to that of another. That is why Emerson wrote, *Imitation is suicide.* When one imitates another, he is canceling himself out. Your goals have to be your own goals.

Creative imagination forms the mold through which the creative process of life works to produce the manifest universe. Whatever man can imagine, man can do.

The Proper Use of Creative Imagination

Everyone is endowed with creative imagination. Creative imagination is using imagination creatively to envision that which we want in life instead of that which we do not want. We all use the mental faculty called imagination, but many of us use it erroneously, imagining ourselves as being poor, unhappy, lonely, or lacking in some other way. Actually, all of the experiences in life,

God is alway at work

Be your unique

Don't be negative

Use your God given talent

those that make us happy and those that we would like to be rid of, have first been envisioned in mind. Experiences come to us because we did entertain some particular mental picture. You see, it behooves us, if we would be happy, to understand something about creative imagination. Otherwise, we may be planting mental seeds from which we do not want the harvest. As Job said, *For the thing which I greatly feared is come upon me, and that which I was afraid of is come unto me.*

Imagination Goes Before Us to Prepare the Way

Albert Einstein once remarked, *Imagination is more important than knowledge.* Why did Einstein consider imagination so important? Knowledge is working with that which has already become a part of our experience. There is nothing wrong with knowledge, but the more we learn the more there is to learn. And so, the mind keeps us moving forward. Imagination, on the other hand, is that which goes before us to prepare the way. Imagination, moving before us, takes us into the realm of the unknown where we are able to use the knowledge we have. Imagination is the outreach of the mind into new experience.

Ralph Waldo Emerson, the sage of Concord, wrote: *Science does not know its debt to imagination.* This is true. Where would the Wright brothers have been had they not been able to imagine

Fear brings bad things upon us.

Never will you know it all

that little plane rising up from the ground. They had to imagine and believe that it could be done. Only then were they able to move forward and work out the details.

There Never Was an Invention Without Creative Imagination

Every great inventor has used creative imagination. Take one of the great inventions of all time, the cotton gin. The inventor was a graduate of Yale University, a young man who liked to tinker. After his graduation from Yale he was invited down to Savannah, Georgia, to visit the home of Nathaniel Green, one of the generals in the Revolutionary War. While there, someone pointed out to him the great problem involved in picking the seeds out of cotton. Have you ever tried to pick the seeds out of cotton? They are embedded in the white fiber and it takes minutes to disentangle just one tiny seed. Cotton, at that time, was costly to produce because man had to manually pick out the seeds.

But leave it to youth. Eli Whitney, just out of college, thought, "This is a problem that must have an answer." Immediately he set out to find the answer. He visualized the seed separated from the cotton. In other words, he put the idea into mind, and soon he began to see that it could be accomplished very simply. Within a few days he had worked out a gadget that was able to clean, in

Imagination is key to success on the creative side.

See it and believe it and you will concieve it

one day, 50 pounds of cotton—an accomplishment that was to the people of that day a miracle! At that time he was only 24 years of age. Thrilled with his victory, he went back up North and set up a factory to manufacture cotton gins. For years his factory was behind in its orders, so great was the demand. Where imagination leads, and is followed with persistence, the goal will be accomplished.

Creative Imagination Has Many Uses

We do not all choose to be inventors. But we can all use creative imagination in many ways. Every part of life in the visible world about us, first had to be an idea in mind. In the beginning of every line of thinking, every chain of mental causation, there has to be the initiator, the place where the idea begins. The chair upon which you sit was first an idea in someone's mind. This idea was translated into a visual image in that person's mind. Out of that image came the final physical expression of the idea. This is why I say, work, in mind, from the end and not the beginning. This may sound a little strange to you because you have heard it said that you start where you are with what you have. But actually, we are saying the same thing, because you really do start right where you are with what you have. It is all a matter of *what do you have?* You have the image of the chair as a finished product. And this is where you begin.

Whatever it is that you desire, when you turn to the inner Source, believe that you receive it, accept it in consciousness, imagine that it is received, and you shall have it. It will surely come into your experience. It is a law that man can do whatever he is able to conceive in his mind, receive in his consciousness, expect with assurance, and accept as happening in his actual experience. The universe does not set our limitations. We set them by our own belief about ourselves.[1]

Creative Imagination in Sports

Creative imagination is an activity of the mind that is a powerful instrument for good. It is a useful tool in so many areas of life. Take golf, for instance. I read in one of Arnold Palmer's columns something that ties in here:

Putting calls for positive attitudes. Lining up, sighting and stroking the putt calls for positive thinking. A negative attitude will tense you up and destroy whatever style you have. To become as self-assured as possible, picture the ball following a proper line to the hole. Do this when you sight the putt, and then retain the image when you are over the ball, riveting your eyes to the back of the ball. Merely hit the ball along the line you have in your mind's eye.

[1]Jack Ensign Addington, *PSYCHOGENESIS*.

✳ Creative imagination can cut strokes from your golf score.

The short-term goal is to put that ball in the hole. Through creative imagination the golfer mentally sets a line upon which to hit the ball. He trusts this line and uses it. His overall goal is to win the tournament. Coincidentally, many other top players have that same goal. Everyone cannot win the tournament. Only one can do that. By using the principles of goal-setting and goal-achievement, one opens the way for victory to become a reality.

Not All Have the Desire to Win

I was interested in reading a newspaper statement by a rookie (first year on golf tour) who stated that very few players on the golf tour actually have the goal of winning the tournament. Many of them have as a goal qualifying for the particular tournament and making the cut. If this is accomplished, then the goal is to be in the money, but not to gain first place. His next statement was very interesting. He said that a great many of them were afraid of the publicity, such as appearing before television cameras, reporters and the public. He said that many could just not imagine themselves in that situation. There are many tour golfers who go strong for two or three rounds and then fade because their creative imagination has not yet taken in the posture of being

Win, Win, Win !

Preech it Brother

victorious. However, some like Jack Nicklaus, Johnnie Miller, or Hubert Green are disappointed if they do not win the tournament. They enter the tournament expecting to win. That is the goal.

Creative Imagination and Universal Mind

In CREATIVE MIND AND SUCCESS, by Ernest Holmes,[1] under the subject, "Using the Imagination," we find this:

Just imagine yourself surrounded by Mind, so plastic so receptive, that it receives the slightest impression of your thought. Whatever you think, it takes up and executes for you. Every thought is received and acted upon. Not some, but all thoughts. Whatever the pattern we provide, that will be our demonstration. If we cannot get over thinking we are poor, then we will remain poor. As soon as we become rich in our thought, then we will be rich in our expression. These are not mere words, but the deepest truth that has ever come to the human race. Hundreds of thousands of the most intelligent thinkers and the most spiritual people of our day are proving this truth. We are not dealing with illusions but with realities; pay no more attention

[1] Ernest Holmes, *Creative Mind and Success*, (New York: Dodd, Mead & Co., 1947).

to the one who ridicules these ideas than you would to the blowing of the wind. In the center of your own soul choose what you want to become, to accomplish; then keep it to yourself. Every day in the silence of absolute conviction KNOW that it is done, as far as you are concerned, as it will be when you experience it in the outer. Imagine yourself to be what you want to be. See only that which you desire, refuse even to think of the other. Stick to it, never doubt. Say many times a day, "I am that thing," and realize what this means. For it means that the great Universal power of Mind IS that, and it CANNOT FAIL.

Expanding Options Through Creative Imagination

By creative imagination we can expand our options in regard to the selection of goals instead of just selecting the obvious. As we expand our consciousness we expand our options. We grow by moving from the known into the unknown. Through creative imagination we do this very thing.

Creative imagination is a creative element in the self-image philosophy. As one imagines himself more creative and more expressive, his expectations will grow and so will his experiences. The architect who is planning a building has to open his mind to all the possibilities that might be beneficial to his client. Here is creative imagination at work. An architect is more than a builder, he is a creative, imaginative artist. His artistic achievements become practical buildings for his client.

Is Creative Imagination Limited to Pictures?

Imagination is not limited to pictures in the mind. Each person tends to think in a way that is unique. The mathematician thinks in terms of mathematics; the artist thinks in terms of color and form; the writer in the terms of the subject in which he is interested, whether it be an abstract or a concrete subject, fiction or non-fiction; the farmer in terms of seeds, weather, harvests. The computer programmer is an example of a person who must be diverse in the use of creative imagination because his thinking has to cover so many various fields of endeavor, and then to creatively convert that knowledge into language that can come through a computer and make sense.

Creative Imagination More Than Daydreaming

Creative imagination is more than daydreaming. One can remake his entire life through an

However you think, think and do it well.

understanding and application of creative imagination. Through creative imagination it is possible to change one's belief about himself and the world in which he lives, thus changing the outer expression of that belief.

It is through creative imagination that man has progressed from level to level of accomplishment and achievement. All forward motion in our civilization has stemmed from the use of creative imagination. Perhaps this is why the Bible states, *Where there is no vision, the people perish.* Creative imagination is the way life creates through man, enabling him to envision in his mind that which he would like to bring to pass in his experience.

Goal-Setting Uses Creative Imagination

Many people set their goals within the range of what has already been accomplished. This is a safe way to go about it. If you do this, you are avoiding the hazards and pitfalls of traveling in a strange country. Such people would be of little value in a brainstorming session.

There is an old saying, *Where we are weakest, there we need stretching.* Creative imagination causes us to stretch, to venture into new areas of creativity. Creative imagination keeps life interesting, opens the way for a wider horizon.

Are you in earnest?
Seize this very moment!
What you can do, or dream you can, begin it.
Boldness has genius, power and magic in it.
Only engage, and then the mind grows heated
Begin, and then the work will be completed.

— Goethe

Some of the quotes
are amazing. I am
learning.

Chapter X

RULING OUT THOSE TREACHEROUS MENTAL BARRIERS

If your goals continually elude you, chances are you have been entertaining mental barriers without realizing it. Those traitors in your mental household seem so reasonable and so familiar, like old friends we have grown up with. But, each one is a snake in the grass, more poisonous than we can ever realize. Mental barriers to goal achievement should be rooted out as soon as possible if we would become goal achievers.

Are Mental Barriers Real?

The best way to approach these rascals is to see them for what they are, phantoms of the night, the bogey-men of your dark thinking. Let's take a long, cold look at some of these traitors:

I'm too young; I can't expect to set the world on fire at my age. "Yes, I can"

Reach for the stars

The sky is the limit

I'm too old; my life is over; I'll soon be retiring anyway.

I'm too stupid; I'm clumsy; I'm awkward.

I don't appeal to the opposite sex; I don't seem to make a good impression.

I'm a slow thinker; I'm sort of dense; anything new baffles me.

I'll never have a good memory; I never can remember names or faces.

Nothing works out for me; what can you expect with my lack of education.

People won't give me a chance because of my race (religion, avoirdupois, politics, etc.).

I never seem to get the breaks.

They're always promoting someone over my head; I never seem to know the right people.

Let's be honest with ourselves. Do any of these types of statements sound familiar? If so, it is important to get rid of them for this is the kind of thinking that keeps us from attaining our goals. It is a form of negative goal-setting that works just as well as affirmative goal-setting. In the last analysis, it is what we believe about ourselves that becomes our experience. While these old familiar statements seem to be good reasons for failure *they are not valid reasons.* They are enemies in the camp but every one of them can be dissolved into thin air *for they only exist in our own minds* as beliefs that tend to bolster our failure patterns.

Believe in yourself

You HAVE too.

How to Overcome Mental Barriers

A person who has lived in a house for some time may go in and out without paying any attention to the condition of the house, the arrangement of the furniture or problems that need correcting. But, let an interior designer in and every problem area will stand out like a sore thumb. The professional will see all kinds of improvements that could be made. Some of us are able to be our own interior designers but it takes objectivity.

The mental house in which we live is very much like our physical house. It, too, becomes cluttered, cluttered with non-thinking cliches and prejudices. Prejudice, as the word implies, means prejudgment, prior judgments, rather than today's judgment. Often we let our mental house become a hodgepodge of limitations and negative patterns. So, the first step in overcoming mental barriers is to get them out in the open and take a good look at them. We need to see them for what they are.

A Mental Inventory Is in Order

What negative ideas are you entertaining in regard to your health? Take a pencil and paper and write out your opinions of yourself in regard to your health. Write out your health habits, and your health patterns. Do any of these constitute limitations or barriers to the good health you would like? Set a goal for healthy living. Think to

Be positive

yourself: "I am healthy. I am strong. I am radiant." Eliminate everything that is not in accord with this. Have the courage to move toward your goal. The barrier can be eliminated. The wonderful thing about life is that each of us has the power of choice, and once we choose a course of action, life cooperates with us to cause the choice to become our experience.

Choose and coperate

Take respondsibility

What negative ideas are you entertaining in regard to your prosperity? Follow the same procedure. Take a pencil and paper and write out your beliefs in regard to prosperity. Are you letting yourself be trapped by one of the following fallacies?

1. It is a fallacy to think that prosperity depends upon luck. _No luck_
2. It is a fallacy to think that prosperity depends solely upon the ability to "get money."
3. It is a fallacy to think that money is evil.
4. It is a fallacy to think that it is wicked to be rich.
5. It is a fallacy to think that it is a virtue to be stingy.
6. It is a fallacy to think that the economic system is faulty and that therefore it is impossible to be prosperous.
7. It is a fallacy to think that the government will take it all away in taxes and that therefore one cannot prosper anyway.

Don't blame
Help out

8. It is a fallacy to think that prosperous living depends upon storing up goods or money for the future.

9. It is a fallacy to think that one is unworthy to receive. *Common*

10. It is a fallacy to think that there is virtue in poverty.

11. It is a fallacy to be a martyr, trying to prove that life is against one.

12. It is a fallacy to think that one has to be grim to be prosperous.

Money is not evil, it is the inordinate love of money that becomes destructive.

When a person prospers he adds to the prosperity of others. He does not take anything away from others unless he thinks that he has to be a thief to prosper. True prosperity is the result of believing that it is right to prosper through the use of the creativity that indwells each one. Eliminate the words *poor* and *lacking* from your vocabulary. Believe it or not, life is *for* you *not against* you. Life wants you to prosper.

Age Is No Barrier

Age is a state of mind. There are young people age 70, old people age 30. The wonderful thing about it is that one can change his mind about himself and become a new person. The life power within each one is ageless. At any age, it can be used in achieving realistic goals.

At the age of 84, Lowell Thomas remarried and with his bride embarked on a new career—a television project in Asia and the Near East.

Leopold Stokowski, at the age of 94, entered into a five year contract with the London Symphony Orchestra to make recordings. He also contracted to direct the orchestra in public on his 100th birthday.

At the age of 66, Colonel Harland Sanders was broke except for Social Security, $105 a month. He decided to do something about it. He remembered his mother's special recipe for fried chicken. He decided to try to sell franchises for marketing her fried chicken formula. After being turned down by scores of restaurants, he sold his first franchise in Salt Lake City. It was an instantaneous hit. Ten years later, at the age of 75, he sold his Kentucky Fried Chicken Enterprise for two million dollars and a substantial lifetime salary. He had set up a series of goals, each goal leading to something greater. Age was no barrier to Colonel Sanders.

In 1972 Ray Kroc and his wife celebrated Kroc's 70th birthday by giving away nine million dollars in McDonald's stock to his employees, and seven and a half million to their favorite charities. At that time his personal wealth was estimated at over five hundred million dollars. Sixteen years before this he was a salesman of mixers used for milkshakes and malts. He sold eight mixers to the owners of a small hamburger stand in San Bernardino, owned by the McDonald brothers. When he looked over their operation, he saw the great possibilities in the way they were doing business. He joined forces with them and shortly thereafter bought them out. By setting goals, he now has restaurants all over the world. He did not consider that he was too old at 52 to embark on a new career. He did not allow mental barriers to impede the high goals he set for himself.

Youth Is No Barrier to Goal-Achievement

A young man approached me following a lecture I gave in New York City. "Do you remember me?" he asked. I had to admit that I didn't. And then he reminded me. He had been a ten year old boy when I last saw him, a boy whose family was discouraging him from his goal of becoming a surgeon. He reminded me that I had told him that while I understood his parents' attitude, there was nothing wrong with his setting a goal and beginning to work toward it. I told him about three of my fraternity brothers at the University of Florida who had had the same goal at his age. They became prominent physicians. He just wanted me to know that he, too, had become a successful surgeon and that he considered his goal to have been a realistic one all through the years, even from the age of ten.

My friend, Dick Bolte, as a very young man had a goal of becoming a millionaire by the time he

Believe and concieve (margin note)

Never, Never give up (margin note)

was thirty-five. He wanted to become a millionaire so that he could devote his life to helping others. At thirty-five he was offered a million dollars for his business which he declined. He sold it at thirty-eight for a million and a half. It was at this point that I met him. He came to see me to discuss how he could best devote his life to helping mankind. I remember a remark he made to me that day. He said, "The thing we've got to do is set up the goals, *no matter how impossible they may seem at the moment, and then start moving toward them.*"

What if Mozart had thought he was too young to write his first symphony at five years of age, or to direct his first symphony at twelve? *Incredible* (margin note)

Albert Einstein astounded the entire scientific world at the age of twenty-five with his revolutionary theory of relativity. *Changed the world* (margin note)

We should all remind ourselves from time to time, that age is no barrier to goal achievement. We're never too young, we're never too old to realize our dreams.

Jack La Lanne's Unusual Goal

I have in my hand a Christmas card from Jack La Lanne. It shows 13 boat-loads of children being towed through Long Beach Harbor by a rope attached to Jack La Lanne. He towed these children for over a mile with his hands and feet bound together. He swam porpoise-like for an hour and 34 minutes. At the end of the swim,

quite an accomplishment (margin note)

[handwritten margin notes: "Not bad for a grandpa" and "Personal is connection good"]

when asked how he felt, La Lanne replied, "Fantastic," and added, "I wanted to prove that 62 is not old."

Author Too Young to Quit Writing at 87

Marguerite de Angeli, after 40 years of writing, is still creating and illustrating children's books which will be read by children for many, many years. Her latest book, WHISTLE FOR THE CROSSING, has just been released by her publisher, Doubleday & Company. Her goal is to continue writing as long as she has interesting stories to tell. Recently she was granted an honorary doctorate by Lehigh University. She is so adept at converting incidents in her life into books that this incident in itself could be the subject of a book.

The Incredible Career of Grandma Moses

Don Wharton, in an article in the Reader's Digest, reported:

> She was 78 years old when she began painting. She had never received a painting lesson, or been inside an art gallery, or had more than a few months' schooling of any sort. Her entire life had been spent on farms, 15 years

of it as a hired girl. Her hands were now arthritic, and she actually didn't know the difference in artistic value between an original painting and a copy of a pretty postcard. Yet a decade later Anna Mary Robertson Moses was one of the best-known artists in the world.

Her career has no parallel. At 90, pictures she had just completed were in galleries and exhibitions in the United States, Austria, Germany, Switzerland, Holland and France. When she reached 100, birthday greetings flooded in from all over the world, including messages from all four living Presidents. When she died in 1961 at 101, it was front-page news across Europe and America. It is only today, with the perspective of a few added years, that we can fathom the full wonder of this fabulous story.

Too often goals are associated with money. Grandma Moses painted pictures for the sheer joy of it. Don Wharton reported that she was keen about being paid a little something for each picture, as if it were a jar of jam, but she was indifferent to large sums. In 1947 her agent sent her a royalty check for $12,000 which she didn't cash. He had to finally visit her at Eagle Bridge and insist that the check be cashed.

She kept learning and improving in her art and hit her stride at around 85. When she was 88 she said, "I can start a batch of five on Monday and

Age is no barrier

have them finished off on a Saturday." She painted more than 1,500 pictures in her last two decades.

When she was 100 she was asked what message she would have for persons in their seventies or older that might help them enjoy their remaining years more. She replied, "I don't know how much good it will do, but I would tell them not to think about growing old or dying. The Lord put us on this earth to enjoy ourselves and we should. They will be happier if they will forget about their age and think about helping others."[1]

Some Goals Sound Crazy to Others—So What?

When I read TWO TOWERS, I WALK, a special feature in Reader's Digest,[2] I thought, "How crazy can a person get!" To think that a young man, 25 years of age, would have the compelling urge to walk on a wire between the twin towers of Manhattan's World Trade Center seemed absolutely insane to me. One hundred and ten stories tall, the twin buildings dwarf the surrounding skyscrapers. One thousand three hundred fifty feet above the ground, and only 131 feet apart. This was an "impossible" feat. The winds flowing between the buildings could blow him off

[1] Parade Magazine, May 1, 1960.
[2] Philippe Petit and John Reddy, READER'S DIGEST, April 1975.

[handwritten in margin: If you put your mind to it anything is possible]

[handwritten in margin: Believe and concieve]

the wire. Also, any sway of the buildings at all could snap the wire cable. Furthermore, all preparations would have to be surreptitious as the owners of the buildings would certainly not give him permission. They could be held liable, if anyone was injured.

Even a helicopter pilot refused to fly between them. But the story I am going to tell you shows what happens when a person sets a goal and believes in it with all his heart.

Philippe Petit first planted the idea in mind when, in 1968, he saw the architect's sketch of these proposed towers in a Paris newspaper. He cut out that picture and playfully drew a line between the tops of the towers, then tossed the clipping into a red stationary box marked "Projects."

In 1973 he glanced through a copy of Paris Match magazine to see a photograph of the actual towers. The steel work was up and the side panels were almost in place. Late in 1973 he went to New York and there he began to plan his surreptitious walk. He visited the towers and managed to escape the guards and other official-looking people by looking official himself. The following day he returned with a friend and took pictures of everything that mattered on the top of the North Tower. Then he returned to Paris.

On May 13, 1974 he flew back to New York and began studying the buildings, mentally planning every step that needed to be taken. He even hired a helicopter and flew over the towers, hovering 500 feet above the top to accustom himself to the height. But when he asked to be flown between the giant pylons, the pilot refused. The winds were too tricky.

He gathered a crew of friends to help him from that time on. He even made a friend of a man who worked on the 82nd floor who helped to make arrangements for putting the equipment into place. It is interesting to note that every time he had a need, someone was there to help him. They were able to get everything into place without anyone in authority knowing anything about it. It was a series of impossibilities made possible through the doing.

On the morning of August 7th, 1974, the great day came. Everything went according to plan. Petit was on the wire for over 45 minutes. Thousands of people gathered to watch this incredible performance. He was arrested by the police immediately afterwards. His "sentence" was to perform for the children in Central Park, which he gladly accepted. No matter what the future holds for Philippe, it is not money that he craves. He seeks, instead, an ideal of perfection.

When you are full of fire, he says, *you can move mountains. When you give everything to your art, you become transformed. I'll never have money in a box, because I want to do things, to start a perfect circus, with only supreme artists for a troupe. To walk Niagara, but not like before, this time, directly over the falls, a mile and more. To suspend a cable to the top of the Eiffel Tower and walk up at a 45-degree angle.*

He'll do it if he believes

Only Your Own Mental Barriers Stand in the Way

Every story I have recounted in this chapter proves that if the elements of goal-achievement are present—desire; determination; focus on the objective; imagination; perseverence; and the will to win, all of life will cooperate with you.

Only you can stand in the way of your goal-achievement providing that the goal is an honest one, realistic according to your own standards. Philippe Petit's goal might not be realistic to you but it was for him. It is in our own minds that goals are won and lost.

all keys of success

Today is the time to begin ridding ourselves of those treacherous mental barriers and move ahead toward achieving our goals.

Today is the day I achieve goals. Today is a great day.

Outline of book

Chapter XI

ALL ABOUT GOALS IN A NUTSHELL

Everyone Is a Goal-Setter Whether or Not He Realizes It

- Some goals are short-range goals, minor objectives, such as hour-to-hour goals and day-to-day goals.
- Some goals are long-range goals, major objectives, that take longer.

Goal-Setting and Achieving Is an Art and a Science

- Goal-achievement works because it is governed by definite mental laws.
- That which we believe about ourselves is sure to become our experience. It is up to us to do our part.
- It is a law of mind that *that which you can conceive of, believe in and confidently expect must become your experience.*

166

- Any system that enables you to mentally release your goals to the creative process of life will aid you in achieving them.
- You can't travel in two directions at once. It is important to keep your mental eye on the goal.
- That to which you give your attention is going to become your experience. This is the mental law of cause and effect.
- Thoughts are things. Your thoughts do materialize.

Either Claim Your Goal or Disclaim It

- If you claim it, you accept it in mind.
- If you disclaim it, you repudiate your right to it.
- Life will take you at your own evaluation.

The Art and Science of Goal-Achieving Can Change Your Life

- It takes the tension and anxiety out of living.
- Once a person understands how to set and achieve goals, his entire life takes a right-about-face.
- Understanding how to achieve goals brings health, wealth and happiness.

Your Mind is Like an Invisible Factory That Constantly Works for You

- It works for you while you sleep.
- You can ask it questions before you go to sleep and wake up with the answers uppermost in your mind.

By Setting Goals We Create a Mold Into Which the Energy of Life Flows

- When we set small goals we provide small molds.
- Our great goals provide great molds.
- The substance of life has been called *mind stuff.*
- *Mind stuff* flows into our mental molds.

The Subconscious Mind Is Like a Willing Servant

- It is the builder of the body.
- It is the seat of memory.
- It draws to you from the Universal Subconscious Mind the ideas that you need.
- The goals you set become orders to the subconscious mind.
- It believes what you tell it and carries out your orders.
- The subconscious mind is the creative medium of the universe acting in and through man.

Every Person Has the Power of Choice

- There is no limit set by Infinite Mind; the individual sets his own limits.
- Each one has the responsibility of choosing his own destination.
- Every time you make a choice you set in motion the Power of the Universe.
- Each thought is a seed planted in the creative medium of life.
- Don't let others make your choices. If you do, you relinquish your God-given freedom of choice.
- Your choices shape your goals.
- Beware of negative choices; they use the same mental principles as your affirmative choices.
- Be careful what you choose for yourself; it will become your experience.

Goal-Setting Gives You a Game Plan— Makes Life Fun

- Making a list of your goals puts them into the factory of life at once.
- Listing our goals strengthens our desires and clarifies our choices.
- Keeping track of goals that are achieved is a good plan because it builds confidence.
- Confidence is the key ingredient of success.
- Listing goals gives us a yardstick by which to measure our accomplishments.

Clipboard Goals Are a Shortcut to Daily Achievement

- When we keep them alive in our heads we tend to worry them, but not do them.
- Each day write down on your clipboard the six most important things to be done that day. Then number them in the order of their importance.
- Work on each goal until it is achieved.
- Cross them off as accomplished.
- A good way of putting first things first.

Persistence Pays Off

- The three P's of goal-achievement are patience, persistence and perseverance.
- Rule out excuses; they are the enemies of goal-achievement.
- Don't allow yourself to become distracted.
- Do not allow yourself to become disturbed by interruptions.
- Don't procrastinate; if you "oughta," then do it!
- Be flexible; be willing to adjust your goals.

Most People Are Too Vague in Goal-Setting

- Vague goals bring vague results.
- Be specific in listing your goals.

The Danger of Unrealistic Goals

- Realistic goals are those you can mentally accept.
- Unrealistic goals are goals with which you cannot identify.

Creating the Right Thought Atmosphere Is of Great Value

- A person's thought atmosphere is the sum total of what he thinks about himself, others and his experience.
- Each one of us creates his experience through his own thinking.
- To succeed in goal-achievement it is important to maintain a positive, affirmative, loving thought atmosphere.
- Hate, fear and anxiety are enemies of creativity.

Rule Out All Condemnation of Yourself and Others

- Get judgment of yourself and others out of the way.
- No one knows what is really best for others.
- It is impossible to judge the right time for the goal to be realized; it probably is on the way.
- Never accept defeat; you may be almost there.

Setting Goals Does Not Mean That We Are Manipulating Life

- Goal-setting gives direction to our lives.
- Goal-setting is a way of selecting an objective and moving toward that objective.
- Goal-setting is an orderly approach to life.

There Are Useful Techniques You Can Use in Goal-Achievement

(See Chapter VII for a complete list.)

1. The technique of choosing a legitimate goal
2. The technique of self-identification
3. The mirror technique
4. The technique of visualization
5. The technique of treasure-mapping
6. The technique of walking in the dream
7. The technique of self-determination
8. The technique of enthusiasm with feeling
9. The technique of self-direction
10. The technique of release
11. Good leadership — setting goals for the group
12. The great secret of goal-achievement: using the Now principle

Now Is the Time to Begin Ridding Ourselves of Those Treacherous Mental Barriers

- It is time for a good mental house-cleaning.

- We must ask ourselves:
  What negative ideas am I entertaining in regard to my health?
- What negative ideas am I entertaining in regard to my business? My home life? etc.
- Age is no barrier to goal-achievement.
- Only you stand in the way of goal-achievement.

Some Guidelines You Can Use to Advantage:

1. Set goals that challenge. Your goals should be mind-stretchers, but not mind-breakers. They should be in accord with your nature. Each one sets his own limits, because goals are personal objectives.

2. Identify with your goal. Be realistic. Don't kid yourself. You can't grow a tail and you know it. Each person should set his own goals. Your goals for another may be something he cannot accept.

3. Your goals should be set in the affirmative.
   Right: "I am free of the smoking habit."
   Wrong: "I'd like to quit smoking."

4. Don't get ahead of yourself. It is never necessary to lie, cheat, steal or injure anyone to achieve worthwhile, realistic goals. Expand your consciousness to the point of believing your goal is already received by you.

5. Beware of goals that are based on envy, jealousy, or false motives. They can only boomerang.

6. Always list your goals in the present tense as if they had already happened. Accept them in the mind NOW.

> Right: "I accept the perfect, right employment for me."
>
> Wrong: "I surely do need a good job. I've been unemployed for so long."

7. Even before you receive the evidence of goals achieved, thank life for causing your goals to become manifest. "I act as though I am and I will be."

8. Life will work with you to the extent that you work with life.

> "It is done to you as you believe."
>
> "As a man thinks in his heart, so is he."

9. Don't set your goal "tongue-in cheek." Be sure you're willing to accept everything that comes with the goal. Example: Are you willing to give up your disability check when health is achieved?

10. The same rules apply to group goals as individual goals: achievement is determined by the intensity of the desire; the unfaltering determination to win; and the consciousness of achieving the goal.